CHRISTI CANADA

Immigrating to Canada vs the USA

Your guide to deciding whether you should immigrate to Canada or America

Contents

1

Immigrating to Canada vs the USA

Your guide to deciding whether you should immigrate to
Canada or America

by
Christi in Canada

* * *

Thanks to Doreen, Ken, Michael and Bev.
Without your help, these words would never have made the
page.

Thanks to Mom and Dad,
Without your gumption, we would never have made it here.

2

Start Here

You are about to embark on one of the biggest decisions you will ever make:

Should I immigrate to Canada... or the USA?

A lot of where you end up in life has a lot to do with where you started as a launching trajectory. I personally believe that where you start your immigration journey can have a huge impact on your income, your investments, your quality of community as well as whether you look back on your life and say "yeah, immigration *was* really worth it!"

This book will give you a real sense of which country would better suit your needs as an immigrant in the long run.

Ultimately this book is a framework, as well as a starting point. (Sorry, I am not a magic eight ball, and can't tell you where you should move.) However, engaging with it should give alternate points of view you haven't considered - as well as a big dose of a long term perspective of life on the "other side".

At the end of each chapter, there will be a set of key questions to help answer which country should better suit your needs, or questions to consider in the life that you want to build in either of these countries.

Make sure to get a pen and paper ready because this is going to be a *highly* interactive ride. You, my friend, are going to have to work to get the full benefit of this book.

I highly encourage you to sit down (with your partner, if you have one) and to go through these sections and write out your responses without judgement and with absolute honesty. You are gathering data and information. Not casting judgement. No one else will ever see these responses. And answering them with absolute candour can help give you the clarity you seek in your decision making process.

These pages also contain immigrant stories, the purpose of which is to show you that where you begin your immigration journey can often frame whether your immigration is ultimately "worth it".

Also, if you enjoy the book, make sure to watch my Youtube channel: Christi In Canada. Even though I reside in Canada, I'm not going to prescribe it as the ultimate location for all immigrants. Your situation is unique.

Disclaimer: Some of these facts and figures in this book are under constant changes. Although I try my best to keep it up to date every 6 months. Please do your due diligence to verify all the facts. I'm only human after all. And if there is something that needs updating, send me an email. It's always nice to meet you :)

3

About Christi

Hey, I'm *Christi in Canada.* I'm your immigration bestie and here to spill the tea on all things related to immigration. With over twenty three years of living in Canada and a popular immigration Youtube channel, I am here to guide you through the process of all the immigration stuff *they don't tell you about.*

I have personally seen how immigration has served me and my family well - as well as watched family members pack up their bags and move back to the "home country." So I care deeply about getting immigration done right, and for the right reasons.

And although I live in Canada, let me tell you I *really* like the States as well. I have family and friends who live there, I travel there frequently and many of my friends are Americans. I come with as little unacknowledged bias as I can.

No, my ultimate goal is to *help you crack the immigration code:*

Help you figure out the immigration options that are best for your unique circumstances, help you bypass paying down the ignorance debt of international inexperience, and be your friend who tells it to you straight - so that you can get to your end goals faster.

4

Kioni's Story

Toronto, Ontario

My phone's alarm buzzes.

It's an early Monday morning in late November. According to the calendar, it is officially still Autumn, but the weather will remain this shade of grey from now till Spring. So really this is just Winter: The extended edition. You can't tell the day has begun because I am living in a basement suite that doesn't really get sunshine. It's a living arrangement that just keeps out enough cold to not let me freeze to death, but maintains a level of damp cold that is only a comfortable temperature for zombies.

Did I mention that I pay over half of my income for the privilege to call it home?

I pull the duvet covers over my head and wish to never leave this bed.

I've been in the country six months, but still sleep on a mattress on the ground. There is never enough time to get an actual bed on the weekend. Because there was never a real weekend when you are working 65 hours a week.

My phone's alarm buzzes. Again. Finally, I muster the courage to get out from under the covers.

In my even colder bathroom, I stand on a mat that's too thin to keep my feet warm. As I move my toothbrush across my mouth my brain goes back to home: Red soil, the never ending sun, the smell of dried grass and the scent of smoke from an open outdoor fire somewhere.

That place seems a world away, and centuries past.

Even the immigration fair I went to just over two years ago, seems like a hazy memory. But I was so desperate to leave Kenya that I was willing to clean toilets to get out of there. So when the immigration agent asked how quickly I wanted to leave, I said "Anything to get onto Canadian soil ASAP!"

Armed with a closed work permit, I stepped onto Canadian soil, anticipating a promising future. I started my job, with dreams of a maple leaf on my passport one day. Little did I know, the workplace harboured a storm in the guise of a boss, Mr. Henderson, a terror in a tailored suit.

At first, I dismissed the subtle warning signs – the relentless demands, the unreasonable deadlines, and the constant pressure to go beyond the scope of the job description. Late nights at the office became routine. Weekends vanished into thin air. While the dreams of a better life seemed to slip through my fingers. I felt utterly trapped by this job that was supposed to be my ticket out of Africa. Mr Henderson dangles the closed work permit in a competitive marketplace over my head.

Cleaning a million toilets would be a welcomed reprieve.

Caught in a web of uncertainty, I brush my teeth back and forth like some form of meditation and prayer. Anything to delay going back into *that* office. While toothpaste foams out of my mouth, tears start running down my face. I can't stop them. I keep asking myself the question: Is it worth enduring this torment for the sake of the Canadian dream, or is it time to admit defeat, pack my bags and return to the familiarity of Kenya?

5

Immigration Options

Immigration can be a nightmare.

Sometimes the desire to get into the country through any means possible seems to be the chant of all immigrants. Because in the end "it will all be worth it!" But there is definitely a hierarchy of immigration avenues - some which offer immigrants more flexibility than others. While other options require way more resources than others to obtain. And others, are quite frankly, a case of indentured servitude for the trade of getting to live in the country.

The best thing you can do is try to find the option that best meets your needs. At worst, you are going through a rough few years meandering through immigration consultant mazes, and working a terrible beginner job (well, the actual worst case scenario is that you don't get to immigrate, or *actual* worse case, you are deported).

Unfortunately, it can mean grinning and bearing it in a tough work situation while you count down the days till permanent residency heaven.

You will also find that the U.S. and Canada have varying routes to citizenship. At a very high level, I've outlined *some* of the immigration avenues of each country. Please note, I didn't summarise every visa option out there, because that could be its own book. Heck, a petit bible even. A very complicated one, with lots of laws.

So, if need be, speak to an immigration lawyer or consultant to see what option best suits you, don't rely solely on this book. The pathways that have been described are general and could change. Consider yourself legally disclaimed.

Canada's Immigration Options:

The Express Entry System:
Starting your journey to Canada via the Express Entry System is like making progress in an intense video game where the stakes are your life; and, the number of points you garner means you win at getting to immigrate. (Considering the last video game I played was Age of Empires, let's see how well this analogy holds up).

Three programs are hosted under the Express Entry system, they are:

- **Federal Skilled Worker Program (FSWP):** This program is designed for skilled workers with foreign work experience who intend to immigrate to Canada

- **Federal Skilled Trades Program (FSTP)**: This program is for skilled tradespersons who have work experience in an eligible skilled trade and want to become permanent residents.
- **Canadian Experience Class (CEC)**: This program is for individuals with Canadian work experience who wish to transition to permanent residence.

The Express Entry game is played at a national level. The game awards points as you create your character (immigration profile), providing information about your age (the highest score is in your twenties to early thirties, decreasing with greater age), education (professional designation, masters level and above scores highest), employment history, and language proficiency. This competition for a higher score and better prospects for advancement results in a competitive environment.

Next, your character enters the Express Entry Pool, a queue where profiles are eager to move forward. The Canadian government, which also serves as the game's organiser, holds draws on a regular basis to choose the characters who score the highest to advance to the next level.

If your character gets selected in a draw, congratulations! You now receive an Invitation to Apply (ITA). It's like receiving a special invitation to move forward in the game. To move forward in the game, you turn in documents at each checkpoint, which serves as evidence of your training and expertise (because no one likes someone who tries to cheat at the game).

Next, a health and background check ensures that your character is fit and that your record is spotless (Your avatar has to reflect reality). This is necessary before you enter Canada. If successful, your character gets Permanent Residence (PR) in Canada. And that's the beginning of the process for citizenship, and how you eventually win the game.

And considering this is a dynamic game, there are ways to level up your chances of getting into the country:

- **Obtain a higher educational level**. To get extra points, finish your Ph.D. or master's degree (like this is some easy feat, I say as I wipe away tears from laughter)
- **Improve your score on language tests** (TEF for French, CELPIP for English, or IELTS for English). Language proficiency testing is something that most Canadian-born Canadians would fail at, but a daunting hoop you as an immigrant must jump through. Make sure to look up Youtube tutorials and practise tests. For the love of all things decent, don't try to "wing it".
- **Obtain further work experience**
- **Obtain a legitimate employment offer** from a Canadian company. If you are asked to pay for a job, this is a scam. Run. But there are some legitimate programs that will have you pay for training and reimburse you after you continued the job for a set period of time (*cough, cough* the aforementioned indentured servitude)
- **Look into Provincial Nominee Programs** (PNPs) in

Canada to receive a nomination from a province, and match your qualifications with jobs that are in demand (more details below).

- **Consult with immigration consultants/lawyers.** Speak with these experts to learn about the positive and negative aspects of your profile and to receive specific guidance. Double check that they are the real deal: That they are legitimate and have a registered number with the College of Immigration and Citizenship Consultants.

Now while this national game is in play, you can also play another version of the game. The end result of getting into Canada is the same, but you drill down more specifically into a province that you would have to meet all the requirements for through the Provincial Nominee Program.

Provincial Nominee Programs (PNPs):

Each Canadian province and territory has its own PNP, allowing them to nominate immigrants with specific skills meeting labour market needs or experiences for permanent residence. Each province and territory has one, except Quebec has its own system (Oui, but of course.)

Express Entry and Non-Express Entry Streams:

Some PNPs are aligned with the federal Express Entry system. Meaning they allow provinces to nominate candidates who are already in the Express Entry pool. This is akin to playing the game at the national level, and while there is some quiet time, you duck into another provincial game and play there, building up scores simultaneously.

Provinces that have PNP aligned with the Express Entry Streams are: Alberta, British Columbia, Manitoba, New Brunswick, Newfoundland and Labrador, Nova Scotia, Ontario, Prince Edward Island, Saskatchewan, and Yukon (also note, you may have some immigration streams in these provinces that are still not aligned with the Express Entry stream. Sorry, I did say that this would be complicated).

While some other provinces have streams *outside* of the Express Entry program. (It's like playing the same game but in a parallel universe, where neither player avatars knows of the other's existence).Those t have PNP outside of Express Entry are: Northwest Territories and Quebec

Occupation-Specific Streams:
Many PNPs have streams targeting specific occupations or sectors facing shortages in the respective province or territory. Check out the occupations for each province you are interested in by some googling.

Entrepreneur and Investor Streams:
And if you have money, Canada will open its doors to you. As long as you are willing to open your purse strings. Or whatever a cryptocurrency is being held in these days. Some PNPs have streams for entrepreneurs and investors who want to establish or invest in businesses.

Family Reunification: Canada places a strong emphasis on family reunification. Canadian citizens and permanent residents can sponsor close family members for immigration. This is great news if you have family legally living in Canada, but completely useless if you don't.

Humanitarian and Refugee Pathways: Canada is known for its welcoming approach to refugees and asylum seekers. The country has a well-established system for refugee resettlement. This has been very popular under the Trudeau administration. But my bets are on this shifting if the Conservatives eventually come back into power.

Student to Citizenship Pathway: Up until January 2024, Canada was actually very open to students becoming citizens, and has a built in journey with permits. However there has been some shifts in this regard to the Post-Graduation Work Permit (PGWP): In 2024, the cap is expected to result in around 360,000 approved study permits, a 35% decrease from 2023. ("Canada to stabilize growth and decrease number of new international student permits issued to approximately 360000 for 2024"). The current political shift favours public universities/colleges over private ones (of which some were essentially glorified education puppy mills - the media's words, not mine). More so, each province will be affected differently as the caps on students will vary.

But the new ruling also offers graduates of master's and other short graduate-level programs eligibility to apply for a 3-year work permit (which is actually a bit of an improvement as the duration of the PGWP used to be equal to the duration of your studies in Canada, up to a maximum of three years.) The PGWP grants international students an open work permit, allowing them to work for any employer and in any occupation of their choice.

Another change is that spouses of international students pursuing master's or doctoral degrees will be eligible for open work permits, not undergraduate programs.

Pick Your Program:	Choose a Canadian school and program you like. Make sure it's one that qualifies for the post grad work permit (is a <u>Designated Learning Institute</u> and not an undergrad program)
Apply and Get In:	Apply to the school, get accepted, and grab that acceptance letter.
Student Visa:	Apply for a study permit (student visa) with your acceptance letter.
Show Your Cash:	Prove you've got the money to cover tuition and living costs.
Background Checks:	You'll need a police check and a medical exam.
Study and Work:	Work part-time, if you can, to help with expenses.
Post-Grad Work Permit:	After you graduate, you might qualify for a work permit
Permanent Residency:	If you want to stay, your time as a student can help with permanent residency

Open vs Closed Work Permits

There are two different types of work permits: open and closed, each with different implications for employment. A holder of an "open work permit" can work in Canada for any employer. That is, it is not job-specific. This flexibility will be particularly useful to foreign students, spouses or common-law partners of skilled workers, graduates of specific Canadian programs, and refugees. Since the open work permits aren't linked to any particular job or employer, their holders are free to explore other employment options.

However, an employer-specific or "closed work permit" limits the holder's ability to work in Canada to that specific employer. Usually, before awarding this type of permit, an employer must demonstrate that a foreign worker is required to fill a particular job position. When an employer wants to obtain a closed work permit, they frequently have to go through the Labor Market Impact Assessment (LMIA) process to make sure hiring a foreign worker won't negatively affect the local job market.

Path to Canadian Citizenship:
After becoming a permanent resident, individuals can apply for Canadian citizenship after a specific period of time. You (and some minors) must have been physically in Canada for at least 1,095 days (3 years) during the 5 years before the date you sign your application. Immigration Canada encourages you to apply with more than 1,095 days of living in Canada in case there's a problem with the calculation.

Following that, candidates must gather supporting documents, such as utility bills, tax documents, and employment records, to demonstrate their time in Canada. The next important step is proving language proficiency in either English or French, as applicants must pass a language test to demonstrate their ability to communicate effectively in one of Canada's official languages.

Furthermore, candidates must pass the citizenship knowledge test, which assesses their understanding of Canadian history, values, institutions, symbols, and citizenship rights and responsibilities.

After satisfying these requirements, candidates can submit their citizenship application, along with the necessary forms and fees. Once the application is received, immigration officials thoroughly review it, including a background check and verification of the provided information. Candidates who pass the assessment are invited to a citizenship ceremony, where they take the Oath of Citizenship (to dear, old King Charles… that still feels weird to type) and officially become Canadian citizens. Yay!

United States' Immigration Options:

Visa Categories: The U.S. has a complex system of visas, including family-sponsored, employment-based, diversity lottery, and humanitarian categories. The U.S. issues green cards (permanent residence) to immigrants, and there are various routes to obtain them, including family sponsorship, employment, and the diversity lottery. In no ways could I capture all the different visas and scenarios, but here are few:

Family-sponsored Visas: Citizens of the United States may sponsor immediate family members for immigration. Parents, siblings, children, and spouses are all included in this. Filing a petition and waiting for approval are the steps in the process.

- **Immediate Relative (IR) Visas**: The 'life's too short for long-distance family drama' visa. These visas are intended for immediate family members of U.S. citizens. Spouses, single children under 21, and parents (if the sponsoring citizen is at least 21) fall into this category. The total number of visas granted in this category per year is not capped.
- **Family Preference (F) Visas**: Because your family is the best 'preference' you can have" visa. A sentiment you can unpack in therapy; not with your immigration officer. This visa allows certain relatives of lawful permanent residents (Green Card holders) and more distant relatives of U.S. citizens are eligible for Family Preference Visas. Four preference groups make up this category: F1 for single sons and daughters of U.S. citizens, F2 for spouses and kids of Green Card holders, F3 for married U.S. citizens' sons and daughters, and F4 for adult U.S. citizens' siblings. These visas are limited and the processing times can be very long.
- **Fiancé(e) Visas (K):** Also known as the visa that brought you the classiest and heartwarming show "90-day Fiance". Americans know how to do entertainment (whether they understand the fundamentals of a healthy long term relationship by dangling a visa - that is another question altogether). The K visa is intended for American citizens' fiancé(e). It allows the fiancé(e) who was born abroad to enter the country with the intention of getting married

within ninety days. The foreign-born spouse has the option to apply for status adjustment after marriage in order to become a permanent resident.

Diversity Visa Lottery: AKA the Green Card Lottery. The U.S. runs an annual Diversity Visa Lottery, allowing individuals from countries with low rates of immigration to the U.S. to apply for a green card. In 2024, 55,000 individuals will get this visa. So yes, the term "lottery" is indeed apt. To be eligible for the DV Lottery, an individual must:

- **Be from an Eligible Country**: Individuals from countries with low immigration rates to the United States are eligible to participate in the DV Lottery. The list of countries that are eligible may change from year to year.
- **Meet Education or Work Experience Requirements:** Applicants must possess one of two qualifications: two years of work experience within the last five years in an occupation requiring at least two years of training or experience, or a high school education or its equivalent, which is defined as successful completion of a 12-year course of formal elementary and secondary education.
- **Submit an Entry**: Participants are required to submit a submission within the designated registration window. One entry per individual is permitted, and the entry process is often completed online.

Employment-based Visas: Those looking to work in the

United States are eligible for these visas. Professionals, investors, and skilled workers can all be sponsored by employers. The list is remarkably long, so I have only earmarked a smattering.

- **H-1B Visa**: With this visa, you can make the American Dream a 9-to-5 reality! This visa is intended for skilled labourers in specialised fields. It is frequently used by professionals in fields like science, engineering, and information technology, and it requires sponsorship from a U.S. employer. Note this visa is not a direct-to-permanent residency option.
- **L-1 Visa:** Why not move up the career ladder while simultaneously moving across continents? Multinational corporations can transfer employees from a foreign office to a U.S. office with the help of L-1 visas, which are intended for intracompany transferees. There are two subcategories: L-1B for workers with specialised knowledge and L-1A for managers and executives. While having an L-1 visa, one can still become a citizen of the United States, but citizenship is not a direct result of the L-1 visa.
- **O Visa:** (The O visa's name honestly feels like a terrible reference to the show "Selling Sunset". Which is the type of trash TV America has utterly excelled in, and that I for one thoroughly enjoy with a glass of wine). Those with exceptional talent or accomplishment in the arts, sciences, business, education, or athletics are eligible for the O visa. It has subcategories such as O-1A for people with exceptional talent in the arts, business, education, or sciences, and O-1B for people in the sciences.The O visa

is a temporary, non-immigrant visa. It is typically granted for an initial period and can be extended, but it does not lead directly to permanent residency or U.S. citizenship.

- **EB-5 Immigrant Investor Visa:**.The EB-5 visa program allows investors to immigrate if they invest a substantial amount of money in a new commercial enterprise that creates jobs. AKA "the pay your way" into the country method costing approximately a cool US$800,000 and taking 5 years of legal residence in the country. They might as well call it the "Hella Rich" visa.

Refugee and Asylee Status: Refugees and those granted asylum may apply for protection in the United States on the grounds of persecution they have experienced in their home countries. Asylum seekers submit their applications from within the nation, while refugees do so from outside. Once in a while I see people post "can I apply for asylum?" when they are not actually under persecution. The answer is no you can't. Feeling persecuted is different than actually *being* persecuted.

Student Visas (F and M): Individuals coming to the U.S. for academic or vocational studies can apply for student visas. The F visa is for academic studies, while the M visa is for vocational programs.There are various steps in the process from a student visa (F-1 or M-1) to U.S. citizenship. Students initially enter the country to pursue academic or vocational studies under the F or M visa, which is usually valid for the length of the student's course of study.

- F-1 students have the option to participate in Optional

Practical Training (OPT) after graduation, which allows them to work in their field of study and obtain useful real-world experience. OPT acts as a transitional program, easing the transfer to other visa categories like H-1B or O-1 visas based on employment offers and qualifications.

- People who look into employment-based visa categories may eventually be able to obtain an EB-2 or EB-3 employment-based immigrant visa, which will grant them permanent residency.

Path to Citizenship: After becoming a Permanent Resident, individuals can apply for U.S. citizenship through naturalisation, which typically involves a waiting period and a citizenship test. The entire process to become a U.S. citizen as an immigrant can take several years, starting from the time you become a lawful Permanent Resident. The timeline can vary based on individual circumstances and immigration categories, but here is the general process:

Eligibility for Naturalisation:

- To apply for naturalisation—the process of obtaining U.S. citizenship—you must fulfil specific qualifying requirements. In general, you need to meet certain requirements and have been a permanent resident for at least five years (or three years if you are married to a citizen of the United States).
- **Filing Form N-400:** To apply for naturalisation, send

Form N-400 to U.S. Citizenship and Immigration Services (USCIS). Including the necessary paperwork and payments.

- **Biometrics Appointment:** Attend a biometrics appointment to provide fingerprints, photographs, and other information for a background check.
- **Interview and English Test:** Attend an interview with USCIS. Your knowledge of English, American history, and government will be assessed.
- **Oath of Allegiance:** If your application is approved, you will be scheduled to attend a naturalisation ceremony where you will take the Oath of Allegiance to become a U.S. citizen. Congratulations you are now American!

The Gist

So, as you can see, Canada and the U.S. have their unique immigration processes, and the choice between the two often depends on an individual's qualifications, employment, family ties, and personal preferences.

Immigration to Canada is generally easier than to the USA, in the sense that Canada has higher proportionate immigration targets relative to the existing population. In 2024, Canada hopes to welcome 485,000 new permanent residents ("Supplementary Information for the 2024-2026 Immigration Levels Plan") which is roughly 1.2% of the country's population as at October 2023. By contrast, America added approximately 1,600,000 new immigrants in 2023 which represented less than 0.5% of the country's population ("U.S. Population Trends Return to Pre-Pandemic Norms as More States Gain Population"). So just because that's a larger absolute number doesn't mean you have a higher chance of success, nor does it mean the process is less complicated.

But, if you are a highly sought after, skilled, professional you will also have a higher chance of being able to obtain visas to either country.

Questions to ask yourself

1. Are you specifically keen on moving to either the U.S. or Canada? Or are you truly open to either equally?
2. Is an immigration option with more avenues to enter the country more appealing to you? (Canada)
3. Or are you willing and able to be in an unknown waiting period for a longer time while you try to get citizenship? (US)
4. Are you willing to go through any avenue possible to just "get there"?
5. Which option out of this section seems most appealing to you? Why?

6

Yasamin's Story

Kansas City, Missouri

The smell of a McDonald's bathroom washes over me: Urinal cakes, bleach, and savagely sweet flowery scented air freshener bombards my nostrils.

And this is a good day for janitorial duties.

In the heart of the American dream, armed with my master's degree in computer science, I find myself tangled in a fluorescent toilet nightmare. My academic laurels, once a source of pride, now mock me as I navigate the unforgiving landscape of the U.S. job market. I used to believe that education was a golden ticket to success. I thought that achieving top academic honours would count for something. But now my naivety makes me seethe. Worst of all, when I finally do get a callback for interviews, it's a cruel joke, because the second they hear my accent, they mark me as an outsider. I never receive a follow up email with the time of the interview.

To make ends meet, I grind away part-time jobs that barely scrape the surface of my financial needs. I am the computer science genius who now finds myself stacking shelves at the GAP as well as a team member at the local Golden arches, a stark departure from the career I envisioned. Tutoring part time is the closest I get to using my skills.

But I still hope that eventually I will get where I want to go. It's the only reason I don't give up.

* * *

Twenty one years later, Yasmina would stand in front of a class full of college students. Teaching part-time at a small community college, getting to do something she loved and finally feeling like she arrived.

7

Work Prospects

Getting your first "real" job after immigration can feel like an insurmountable task.

For some it takes years to reach that milestone. Often when I speak to would-be immigrants they have a sense of believing that they will be the exception to the rule. They believe they will get a job sooner than most. That their amazing work ethic alone will make them stand out from the masses. They don't realise how long the road in front of them may be. That they are at a fundamental disadvantage compared to their non-immigrant counterparts. Even if you had a more advanced degree than your Canadian counterpart, when you land with no social network and no local experience, you are essentially starting at zero. When you start from an "empty network bank account" - It means that your first few jobs may not be close to the career options you had in mind.

This type of post is one that I see regularly in immigration groups:

facebook

Create story

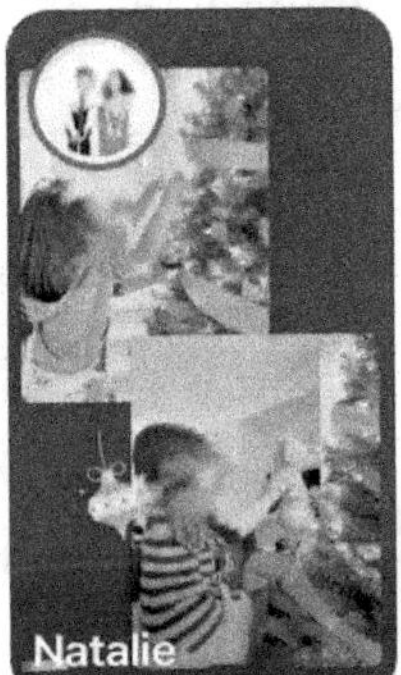

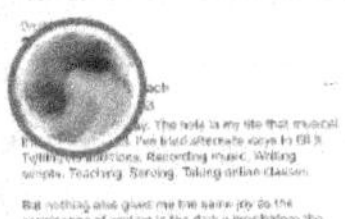

Anonymous member · 2h ·

Finding a job! Why is it so hard to find a "normal" job? The only people interested employing me is in retail (Walmart, Target etc) working over weekends and stupid hours. I have 10 years experience in accounting but not with quickbooks. I was interviewed once and she laughed at me when I explained my experience. I have no confidence when speaking because it feels like they never understand me. Feeling discouraged! I surely didn't come to the USA stocking grocery isles. (Current job) I have been applying for intro jobs like reception but nothing! Suggestions welcome!

😀👍 27   76 comments

 Like    Comment    Send

In both countries, landing a job often involves searching, networking, and adapting to the local job market. It's important to research the specific requirements and job opportunities in your field, as well as the region you're interested in. Your qualifications, visa status, and local job market conditions will play a significant role in your success in either the USA or Canada.

To increase the chances in either country, I would get very strategic and learn the ins and outs of the local job market.

Personally, I would:

- Make sure my resume speaks to the market I am in. I would hire a resume writer if I was getting no bites after a few months.
- I'd search for someone on Linkedin for someone in my field in the geographic location I was thinking of moving to and ask them for an informational interview over zoom. (I have some other youtube videos and content that covers that). An easy break the ice method I have used is to find old immigrants from my home country and ask them for coffee to hear how they did it.
- I would clearly articulate my ask: 15 minutes of their time, outline the questions I would like answered so there are no surprises.
- I would **not** ask them for a job, there is nothing that would make it more awkward and make them wish they didn't take the call than asking for a job.
- I would ask them if they had any more contacts in the field who would be willing to have the same chat with me

(usually people do, and are happy to do an intro)
- And I would get out there and connect in person wherever I could. This can be the most intimidating feeling when you are not having success in your job hunt. But incredibly helpful.
- And again, remember, this may take a heck of a lot longer than you ever thought it would

All these things can really help your job hunting, but here are the specifics that pertain to each country:

Canada Work Prospects

- Canadians are obsessed with Canadian experience, if you don't have Canadian experience especially in the field you work in it makes it ten times harder to get a position
- Sometimes, Canadian jobs are lower paying than the U.S. counterparts. It really depends on the industry but for the highest paying jobs, people go to the US.
- Canada generally has a higher rate of unionisation, more supportive labour laws, and a stronger influence of unions in some key sectors like healthcare and education. But getting into the union can also not be the easiest thing if you are coming from the outside.
- Canada is also very particular about its professional associations. Do not be surprised if you end up repeating the exact same courses you did in your home country, in Canada, *just to get the Canadian credit.* Just so you can join the association or professional body. Hoops. Gotta love 'em.

- Canada has federal and provincial labour laws that protect workers' rights. While labour laws vary by province, they tend to provide more comprehensive support for workers, including healthcare, parental leave, and paid vacation.

USA Work Prospects

- Americans are generally more open to non-Americans getting positions (especially if you are a Canadian immigrant).
- There is also higher remuneration for high skill and in-demand jobs in America. (Except in the case of school teachers, for some reason America dislikes paying them)
- Labour laws in the U.S. are a mix of federal and state regulations. Employment standards and workers' rights can vary significantly from state to state. Federal laws, like the Fair Labor Standards Act, establish minimum wage and overtime standards. But expect lower minimum wages in the U.S. compared to Canada.

The Gist

The intensity of the job hunt will completely depend on your skill set and the demand for your skills.

I have some Canadian friends who are highly-skilled, who ended up working in the US. It afforded them the opportunity to make a lot of money and work at some really large companies in the IT space. But then I've also known immigrants to the U.S. who weren't highly skilled, and found working in the

U.S. was really a grind. It was ultimately difficult for them to " move up" in life.

As a general rule, if you are a highly skilled individual, *and* sought after in your abilities, you can win big in the US! However, if you have more "normal skills" (I, dear reader, fall 100% into this category, so no judgement if you keep me company!) and are not going to be working in highly specialised fields of employment you *may be* in a better economic situation overall in Canada.

Christi's Two Cents

Although this book is a comparison between the States and Canada, as an immigrant I want to impress on you the idea that looking for work in a new country is just going to be a plain hard thing to do. (Sorry, I keep repeating this, but honestly you may need to hear it several more times).

Resetting expectations is probably one of the most helpful things you can do. Finding a job in either country could be its own book let alone a section. But here are a few important thoughts to leave you with:

- There are cultural, industry and positional differences when applying for jobs in North America. Here, to-the-point resumes and cover letters are the norm. You are shooting yourself in the foot if you don't learn to adapt your experience into the culturally appropriate approach.

Overall, as we enter a brave new world of AI, I'd consider using these tools to your advantage and increase the volume of shots you take and jobs you apply for:

- Use AI to rewrite your resume and you can be the editor who fine tunes it. There are many tools out there: but here is one to get you started: https://www.kickresume.com/en/ai-resume-writer/
- If you have the funds and are mass job hunting, tools like this one can help you save time https://lazyapply.com/, through the mass applying approach (full disclosure: I have not personally used it, but the concept seems amazing). Which if you are playing a numbers game can make sense. Although, There are some jobs that require a sniper's precision in their application, use your discretion as to which category you fall under.

Questions to ask yourself

1. Are you in a highly specialised field (think specialist doctor, in demand lawyer, engineer, CFA, healthcare worker) which puts you in a position to earn a high income? (USA or Canada)
2. Do some internet sleuthing: What is the average income for the role you are looking for in the industry you ideally

want to work in? Run the numbers for your partner as well.

3. Click the links and do a high level calculation on the amount of tax you may be paying on your income. (You will need to choose a province/state to get a more accurate picture, also these are third party sites and I don't control the content on them.)

Canada: Click here.
USA: Click here

1. Is it important to you to maximise your income over other factors of living? (USA)
2. Do you have more "transferrable" skills, AKA are you ok with a potentially lower income? Or would you be more comfortable with government support to maintain your standard of living? (Canada)
3. Do you see yourself working as an entrepreneur? That is, building a business that requires access to a large market of talent and consumers, not just self employment/contract work. (USA or Canada, depending on the industry)
4. Which option in this section seems most appealing to you? Why?

8

Saanvika's Story

Saskatoon, Saskatchewan

It was February in Saskatchewan. Which means "damn cold" is the understatement of the century.

I held onto my brand-new healthcare card. It had arrived in the mail three days prior. I never thought that at age twenty-seven I would *actually* have to use it. It is more like a friendly Canadian list of things you receive as you come to land:

✔Customs and Immigrations
  ✔World's warmest coat
  ✔Move into a funky-smelling AirBNB

But here I am lying on the ground of the apartment, and I am praying that this card actually means I can see a doctor at no cost.

I keep thinking: *This can't be happening.*

It feels as if my heart has thunder in it. It palpitates so hard and so erratically I wonder if anyone else can hear it.

Is this a heart attack? An anxiety attack? Actual heart failure? As a newcomer, I hesitate. I know that the healthcare system should cover this, but would it, *like actually cover it?* Am I too new? Would they revoke my Permanent Residency because I came here under the guise that I was healthy?

But I have to do something. So I test the waters. I dial the nurse's help line.

"Call an ambulance," they urged.

The word 'ambulance' echoes like a tolling bell in my mind. I am walking a fine line of just making ends meet. A bill - I feared. Or a missed shift at work which would lead to a financial storm. I couldn't even qualify for a credit card yet. My emergency money cushion was almost non-existent.

As the ambulance roars outside. And two of the most burly Canadian looking men moved me onto the stretcher. But I feel so scared and so alone. The rest of the journey is just a blur until I am under the hospital lights, amid beeping machines, my healthcare card tucked into my pocket.

A few hours later, my heart rate had calmed down. I have to see some specialists. But I am out of imminent danger. Yet the fear of payment is a tempest in my mind that refuses to go away.

Minutes tick by, each one anxious. But then, I was told I could go home.

I felt the stress rise as I walked out, I was wondering when someone was going to pull me aside and say "you need to pay, young lady!"

But there was no one. There was no bill. The weight of my worry lifted, replaced by a flood of relief. I stood there, under the stars of my new home, tears streaming down my face… until I realised if I kept crying I would be wiping ice from my face. So I hurried my grateful butt home.

9

Health Care Insurance

There are few things that get Canadians and Americans as fired up as the debate around *their* healthcare system- and which country has it better or worse.

If you ever want to set off a little emotionally-ladened-rhetoric-filled bomb: Ask an American or Canadian what they think about their healthcare in the *other country* - and watch the fireworks.

My hope is to cut through the emotions, the rosy coloured glasses, and the hyped-up emotionalism and to rather give you a sense of what you are getting yourself into, in either nation. With a smattering of some real stories for extra measure,

Canadian Healthcare:

We have a concept here in the Great White North called "Universal Healthcare." It acts as a superhero, providing healthcare to all citizens and permanent residents. However, it is an ageing superhero who must deal with the shifting winds of governance, the practicalities of a budget, as well as damn terrible PR:

Here's the rundown of what to expect:

- The provinces are in charge. This means that healthcare is managed differently from province to province or territory to province. Sorry, but this isn't consistent across the board.
- It's a single-payer system. The government's like your one-stop-shop for healthcare bills. So there's no need to whip out your wallet for doctor visits and hospital stays.
- It's all funded by taxes. Canadians chip in to make sure healthcare is accessible to everyone. It's kind of like a big family potluck, but for healthcare.
- Your friendly neighbourhood family doctor is a big deal. Like a really big deal. Primary care and preventive medicine are highly valued in Canada. Your family doctor is your gatekeeper to the specialist world. But, finding a good family doctor can be a big pain in the arse, and take a long-ass time (sorry, I'm no proctologist). Like years to get into the books, or be stuck in walk-in clinic purgatory. Sorry to be the bearer of bad news.
- Here is the kicker, Canada's universal Healthcare does not cover dental care (well not yet again, there is a new plan under way for lower income individual and seniors), nor eyecare (that is glasses with corrective lenses are a no, cataracts and other more intensive issues are covered) or most prescriptions. So, It's not as universal as you would

think. However, if you are employed, most employees have a relatively decent extended healthcare plan that can help take the sting out of the out of pocket costs.

- Also, extended healthcare costs can vary from province to province. What is a tolerable dental cleaning expense in British Columbia can cause a heart attack in Alberta.
- If your medical situation is not urgent or critical, the wait times for service can be long. So, so long.

Especially for specialists:

Averaged over all 12 specialties and 10 provinces surveyed, the total waiting time between a general practitioner's referral and the specialist's provision of medically necessary elective treatment has increased from 25.6 weeks in 2021 to 27.4 weeks in 2022. The wait time for 2022 is 195% longer than it was in 1993 with a wait time of 9.3 weeks. (Moir and The Fraser Institute 1) I wasn't kidding about the healthcare system being like an ageing superhero, who is moving slower.

But what type of Healthcare coverage can I get as an immigrant?

This is a bit of an "it depends" scenario: but Permanent Residents, Protected Person, temporary residents with valid work or study permits (varies by province) have access to the universal healthcare plan.

Some provinces require newly arrived immigrants to wait before becoming eligible for provincial health insurance. The waiting period varies by province and can last anywhere between a few days and several months.

This includes International students and temporary foreign workers: They may have limited access to provincial health insurance. Some provinces may demand proof of private health insurance coverage or the purchase of private insurance plans. As well as Refugee applicants: While refugees have access to essential and emergency healthcare, they may face restrictions on non-urgent medical services. When their refugee claim is approved, they are usually eligible for full provincial health coverage.

USA Healthcare:

American Healthcare is the Land of Choices:

- In the good old U.S. of A, it's like a healthcare buffet with options galore. It's a mix of public and private players. But it's not an all you can eat buffet, so hold onto your wallet, before you preload your plate.
- There's no universal coverage here. It's like a choose-your-own-adventure book where not everyone gets a happy ending. Some folks have insurance, some don't.
- Employment and insurance go hand in hand. Many Americans get their healthcare coverage from their jobs. But if your job doesn't serve up insurance, you're on your own. Like you are setting up a gofundme page and asking

internet strangers to help you out.

- Brace yourself for the "out-of-pocket" rollercoaster. Co-payments, premiums, deductibles - it's like navigating a financial maze. You pay as you go.
- Uncle Sam's got some programs up his sleeve, like Medicaid for the low-income crowd and Medicare for the seniors. But there are holes in the safety net.

Medicaid and Medicare

But wait, Christi, you just mentioned some programs that cover healthcare in the states?

Ok, you got me:

In the United States, Medicare and Medicaid are two government-sponsored healthcare programs that serve different populations and have distinct eligibility criteria, coverage, and funding structures.

Medicare

Medicare, a federally funded program, mainly serves people 65 and older, as well as some younger individuals with qualifying disabilities. Medicare is generally available to those over the age of 65, with automatic enrollment in many cases. Individuals under the age of 65, on the other hand, may be eligible if they have previously received Social Security Disability Insurance (SSDI). Criminal convictions, particularly for healthcare fraud, can disqualify individuals from getting Medicare.

Medicare covers a range of services through different parts (A, B, C, and D), including (A: hospital stays), medical services (B: outpatient care, doctor visits, preventive services, and some home health care). Medicare Advantage plans (C often includes additional benefits like vision and dental coverage), and D: prescription drugs. However, it does not cover certain services like long-term care.

Medicaid

Medicaid, on the other hand, is a federal-state partnership program that provides healthcare coverage to low-income individuals and families, including pregnant women, children, the elderly, and the disabled. Eligibility mainly depends on income and family size, with certain groups automatically qualifying. Individuals with greater financial resources may not be eligible for Medicaid.

Income or family status changes can have an effect on Medicaid eligibility, and increased income could end in disqualification. Medicaid covers a wide range of health-care services, such as hospitalisation, doctor visits, preventive care, and long-term care. In some cases, Medicaid does not cover the same services as Medicare, and the specifics vary by state.

But isn't that like universal healthcare, Christi?

No, because - to not put it politely - you either have to be a senior or poor to qualify, or have a disability. Plus, due to financial constraints, millions of Americans remain uninsured or underinsured.

The fragmented nature of the American healthcare system, which consists of a combination of public and private insurers, employer-sponsored plans, and health insurance marketplaces created by the Affordable Care Act (ACA), is another reason it isn't universal. Disparities in access and benefits are still present.

But what type of Healthcare coverage can I get as an immigrant?

You will need to get private healthcare for or health insurance through your employer if you are on a visa.

Medicaid is available to people who are not citizens of the United States (Sigh of relief). That is, legally residing immigrants, including those with green cards (legal permanent residents), may be eligible. But, it has some clauses: It depends on your immigration status, date of entry, and state of residence. Certain immigrants, particularly those who obtained a green card through family sponsorship, may be required to wait before becoming eligible for Medicaid.

Rather than citizenship status, Medicare eligibility is typically determined by age (65 or older) or certain qualifying disabilities. In general, Medicare is available to legally residing immigrants, including those with green cards. Immigrants who have lived in the United States legally for at least five years are usually eligible for Medicare. However, for those who meet specific criteria, such as having a qualifying work history in the United States, this waiting period can be waived.

File this specific question and my answer under "I am going to have to do research to figure out my unique situation."

The Gist

Canada's Healthcare is not perfect by any means. However, it will be there if you need it. When exactly you need it, is another question. The thing with the USA, is that if you have money you can get a lot of great things come your way - and excellent Healthcare - is one of them. The only thing is you have to have money, and ample amounts of it. Or poor and in the right age bracket.

The other thing worth noting. If you have oodles of money and you are a Canadian, you can still pay for private healthcare in the USA. The wait times would be much quicker and you would be able to proverbially "skip the line" in Canada. You will just be paying twice (once through your taxes) and again for the actual service.

Christi's Two Cents

Some of my extended family live in the United States. And their experience of the Healthcare System - especially as they have aged - has been… rough. Healthcare is expensive because you are ageing, and you need more healthcare use as you… well, age. However, it's usually the time in life when your income is declining, as you have entered into retirement. So it becomes a real catch-22, with your health in the balance.

But even if you are not older or have any underlying conditions, sometimes, life just happens. I was scrolling through one of the immigrant groups that I follow online. And I saw this post from an immigrant:

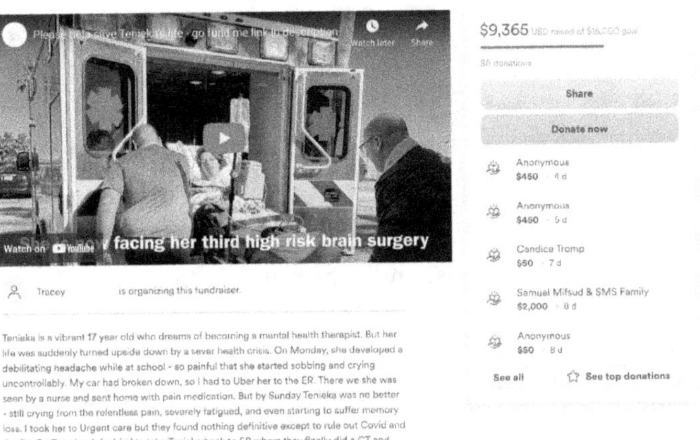

Her teenage daughter was in need of an operation to help save her life. Even with employer's healthcare insurance, there were still "massive medical bills" that needed paying. She was hoping to raise $15,000 and reached out to all communities she could for support.

Her story is heartbreaking, and sadly not uncommon. Here is another:

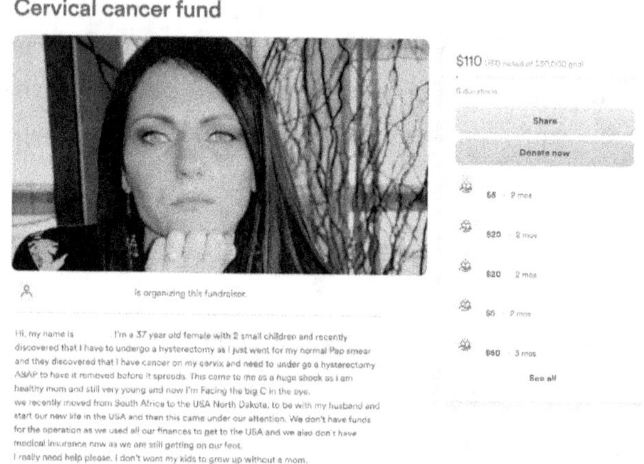

An immigrant who found cancer while they didn't qualify for coverage from her husband's insurance.

As I scroll through the hundreds of requests on GoFundMe's homepage. I am moved by Americans' kindness and willingness to give to those who are in need.

I share these stories not to vilify the USA's system but to show that there are real people who end up needing help. Which is often all of us at some point in our lives. Because we aren't gods or superheroes, we age and break down.

Anecdotally, I've had an incredible experience with the Canadian Healthcare System including birthing two children. As have all of my chronically ill family, including kidney transplants, cancer treatment, and strokes.

But I am not going to make like its a bed of roses here:

I have also definitely sat in the Emergency Waiting Room for several hours with my kids when they had a terrible stomach bug. They were not dying, nor in a critical state, thus the wait was long because triage (a fancy french word for assessment and prioritisation) determined that our conditions warranted being lower on the list. However, I couldn't get to see a walk-in doctor to make sure that things were not going sideways, and the nurses' helpline (yes, that is a real thing) recommended I get them checked out. So there we waited.

Again in a similar vein, I have heard stories from fellow moms about the long wait time for services for their young children that are again important to the child's development, but that such high demands that there are no immediate openings or appointments so you end up waiting a few weeks or months to see a specialist. Which as a parent, can be absolutely frustrating.

While another of my family members has been on a two year wait list for a hip replacement, with no updates of a potential date in sight. He has been seeing his doctor regularly as well as finding alternative methods to try and deal with the pain. But ultimately, the replacement is the only thing that will help him get better and let him go on with this active life.

Questions to ask yourself

1. How young are you; and, how healthy are you? (If on the healthy end of the spectrum, both countries may be acceptable to you.)
2. Do you have, or does your family have a history of chronic illnesses? If you have a sense that you may have some healthcare issues in your future, because genetics handed you a tough hand. (Canada may be a better place to park yourself).
3. Do you have a surplus of money to cover accidents or additional medical bills? How much can you set aside (or keep in liquid assets)? (USA)
4. Do you plan to have children via a direct birth (as opposed to adoption)
5. Do you plan to work as a contractor or entrepreneur at some point? Do you have a plan in place to have insurance to cover any potential health costs?
6. Which option in this section seems most appealing to you? Why?

10

Arun's Story

Los Angeles, California

My phone buzzes. The voicemail icon for a missed call appears.

Immediately my hands are clammy and I can feel my voice box tighten.

This is it. It's do or die time. It's the culmination of four years of studying, four summers of internships and five rounds of interviews at Google. *The* Google. Or as my mother would correct me: "Alphabet is the parent company. How are you going to get a job there if you can't even get the name right, Arun?"

Why did I miss the voice message?! Why did I have to pee at that moment? Why did I think a Venti Caramel Swirl Frappuccino could ever be a good idea?

The icon is still on my phone. The number one in a bright red box. Like a small little birthday gift… It had to be good news right? They would have emailed with bad news, right?

I know that once I listen to this message I can't unhear it. The point of no return. The big gamble of get "Arun to America so that he can study and get an amazing job" either pays off right now, or I am going to do some career version of the walk of shame all the way back to Sri Lanka.

Or worst of all, I was going to have to tell my mom that "no, I did not get it". And then what? Where would I turn to after that? Moving back home to try and meet a nice girl, and get married?

What if it wasn't a phone call from Google?

What if it was my mother, and something had happened to her, and now even if I got the job, I would have to move back home to go look after her. If I didn't do that, would I be a terrible son? Or would my mother feel terrible because she made me miss out on an opportunity of a life time?

In one fell swoop I slurp back the last bit of the lukewarm frappuccino. It tastes disgustingly sweet now. While the sugar rush hits me I hit the voicemail icon and tap in my pin with shaky fingers.

"Hi Arun, this is Caitlyn from HR, I wanted to follow up from our earlier interviews. And thank you so much for your time. As well as invite you to formally join the team!"

There is not enough air fist pumping in the world to represent how happy I am at this very moment.

11

Post Secondary Education

Opting for post-secondary education for a promising future is like following a script so tattered that the lines are barely legible.

Yet it is a narrative that most native Canadians or Americans still believe in. And 1.4 million Canadians head into school each year ("Facts and stats"). While a whopping 15.4 million students in America do the same ritual.("COE - Undergraduate Enrollment"). And it's such a powerful narrative that immigrants will go to extreme lengths to get into prestigious colleges, all in the hopes of it leading to a prestigious well paying job.

And the reality is, sometimes it can still really work out. And in the worst case scenario you still have a great education to fall back on.

But, and this is a big but, the level of debt you take on to obtain an education is a calculated risk: Factors of academic success, future potential income, job market demand, and good old luck all play into it.

So let's dive into the different options each country provides you.

Canadian Post Secondary

In Canada, diversity in education is akin to selecting from a range of institutions – universities, colleges, and polytechnics – resembling a varied menu of learning options.

- Tuition is often kinder on the pocket. It's like buying a nice meal at a local restaurant, not a fancy downtown joint. But prices can vary depending on the province. If you are Canadian or a PR, you can spend about $6000 - $7000 CAN on tuition per year for an undergraduate program. Except in Quebec, they have some weird rules there, which are quite frankly beyond the scope of this ebook. (In general, assume anything that surrounds the French language *in Canada* as hella confusing, drowning in bureaucracy, and dancing in some special grey zone of special conditions).

- Scholarships and grants are plentiful, making it easier to score some financial help. Provinces and schools often join the giving party, so it's like getting surprise gifts.

- But if you are an international student you are going to have to triple to quadruple this price point. Argh, brutal. I hate to say it, but I personally think that there is a bit of an "academic industrial complex" when it comes to post-secondary institutes recruiting and bringing in international students. That is, Institutions need these students to justify their own existence, and these students pay to play.

American Colleges

In the USA, there's a smorgasbord of colleges and universities to pick from. It's like a massive shopping mall for education.

- Tuition is where things get a bit spicy. Private schools can be as expensive as a fancy sports car, while public schools offer a discount for in-state students. Out-of-state students, though, pay a premium.
- The average *annual* tuition for American schools:
- $10,230 (in-state students at a four-year public college)
- $26,290 (out-of-state students at a four-year public college)
- $$35,830 (private non-profit four-year college)

And that's not even getting into the price for international students. Poor souls.

- Scholarships and grants are like hidden treasures. You might need a map to navigate the financial aid maze. The

FAFSA form is your golden ticket, and you may have to do some treasure hunting for scholarships.

But It is worth noting America also is home to some of the most prestigious institutions in the world. And if you graduate from those universities you might land up in a prestigious job or be well-connected to the right network of people who can open doors for you.At least, that is the hope.

The Gist

You will get a much more affordable post secondary experience in Canada. In some cases up to a quarter of the tuition cost in the US. Plus, Canada's student loans people are much kinder. They even forgave some of my debt right off the top at the end of my degree. How polite.

And honestly, you will get an equal level of education from both countries. You really just have to look up the top universities for the best quality of education.

Christi's Two Cents

A word of the wise and from my personal experience, for an undergraduate degree I would personally try to attend a Canadian institute that is a) a public institute, not private b) one that has been a university for a while. Out of personal experience, I have done a degree at a larger institution which had much more academic rigour, and then a college-turned-university situation (it was a bit more hit and miss on the quality of the instruction).

Questions to ask yourself

1. Are you a verifiable genius, and have you utterly crushed your academic goals? If you, a lot of doors can open for you in both countries. If you have stellar grades, as well as enough leadership to steer the vision for a small country, you too could be rewarded with scholarships galore, and again, both countries can provide you an opportunity to study. (USA/Canada)
2. Do you have a particular program in mind? What is the total tuition for the program?
3. Do some comparison shopping, and see how much that program would cost you in either Canada or the United States. Note them here:
4. Are you studying a degree with a clearly lucrative path post graduation? How much do you expect to earn in your first year? (USA)
5. Are you studying at an institution that has a lot of cache with the lucrative industry you are trying to get into (E.g an engineer looking to get into Silicon Valley)? (USA)
6. Are you studying a more general degree with less lucrative prospects? (Canada)
7. Are you looking to use your education as a means to gain permanent residency in that country? (Canada has some more clear pathways to do just this)
8. Do you have children who are considering attending a post secondary institution in the near future?

9. If so, what are the expectations for you helping them out with their education expenses? Immigration can take a bite out of your savings and earning potential for a while, have you clearly mapped out what you can afford?

10. Which option in this section seems most appealing to you? Why?

12

Free Goodwill

There is also a special place in my heart for all immigrants; specifically, those who help out someone new to the land.

I don't tell this to people, butI say a little prayer every time I see a big plane fly overhead.

"God, please help the immigrants who are setting foot on this land for the first time. Please let them be welcomed here".

I have done introductions, fielded dozens of calls from would-be immigrants, asked for expert insights for other immigrants, and made youtube videos about your deep burning immigration questions.

I don't do this for accolades. I do this because immigration is freaking hard.

It's even harder when other immigrants don't want to lend

a helping hand. And I think we all have it in us to help one another on this wild and wonderful journey.

So I am going to ask for a bit of help from you:

One immigrant to another, asking for a favour: If you find this book helpful, could you please take 60 seconds and leave it a review on Amazon?

Your words can help another immigrant find clarity when they feel hopelessly overwhelmed by a huge decision.

And thank you. I truly appreciate it.

13

Saoirse's Story

Hoboken, New Jersey

Leaving my hometown of Kilkenny in Ireland to pursue stand up in America may have been a joke to my family, but to me, it was the ultimate dream. They all asked, "why don't you just go to London with the rest of the wannabe actors?" But I knew that if I could make it in America, it would translate to success worldwide.

Plus, in America, my accent was a novelty. Bonus.

So I made it to the States and started working the stand up routines in whatever late night cafe would take me. I was doing this for months, while working my survival "Joe Job" in the daytime. I was starting to get some regular spots, and even got chatting with a talent agent. She liked my work, and enjoyed my point of view. I was just on the cusp of feeling like things were going to move my way when she asked "what type of following do you have?"

Let's be clear here: I didn't have a social media following. I wasn't planning on becoming internet famous. I wanted to be famous-famous. The type of famous, where I can afford to eat Taco Bell anytime I want, not because it's all I can afford.

The agent smiles. She picks up her phone and pulls up a hugely popular comedian's social account. She plays me his top reel and says "This one. This one is the reason he has a Netflix special"

So it turns out, internet fame counts for a lot. She told me to call her once I had my first 10,000 followers.

No sweat, right?

So I start making reels about my different routines. But the reels don't get many views. Like none. And mostly it's my poor sister who is doing all the liking. Bless her soul.

All except one reel, it's the bit where I talk about being Irish in America.

I have struck my leprechaun's pot of gold. It's time to dig a little deeper.

I decided to lean in heavily and create a whole routine about it. I poke a little fun where I say being an immigrant in America is like being in an emotionally abusive relationship, and everytime I go through Irish immigration and customs they question me like it's a mental health check:

"Mam are you ok?"

And I respond "You just don't know him (America) the way I do!"

When I do the bit in real life, the laughs in the room are *chef's kiss*.

And the reel version of it, gets a lot of likes and views. But it also gets a lot of hate. Multiple people leave comments on the same vein with varying degrees of civility, "that if you don't like it, don't let the door hit ya on the way out!"

Things people would never say to me in person, they hurl over the internet.

It's a damn comedy routine, and people are losing their minds.

Just because I use humour to highlight what it is like to be an immigrant in America? It's as if I didn't say all the time how grateful I was to be in America and how wonderful it was, then I wasn't worthy of being here.

And I can't help but think to myself: I am literally from some of the palest people on the planet, and I am told to shut up with such vitriol? What about anyone who doesn't look like me?

14

Openness to Newcomers

When it comes to the internet, you have to take the comments section with a grain of salt.

As someone who runs an active Youtube channel, I have had some really fun comments come my way:

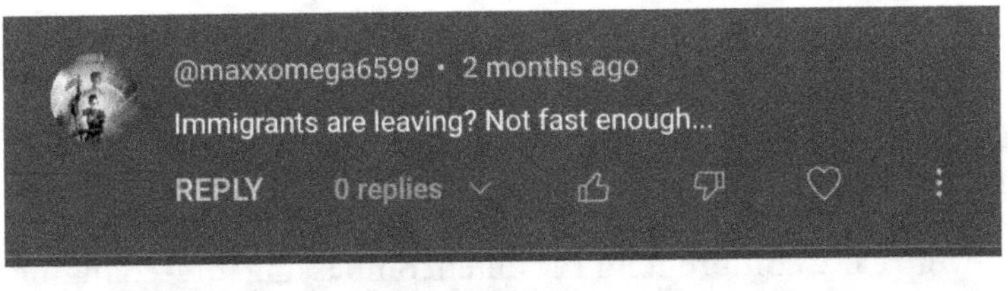

And although I believe that these are oftentimes people's most true and sometimes meanest musings (which they post from the comfort of an anonymous keyboard.) I also don't think most people have the courage to say those things to my face. Real life cowards -t hey give me hope. Real life vitriol, that makes me uneasy.

But I tell you this, not to make myself feel better, but to heed a warning: *People who have never gone through immigration can never know the toll that the journey has taken.* And speaking your truth - and it is true - about your immigration experience to them is like explaining is like trying to feed books to fish: No matter how well-intentioned, the substance remains irrelevant in their aquatic world.

Obviously there are some people who are kind hearted and truly care (hold onto them, and potentially marry them). But for many it's just an experience so far removed that they can never really comprehend the all encompassing, life-changing journey that is immigration.

But what does the general public think of newcomers?

Canada

Canada has the "Multicultural Mosaic" concept as the backbone to its immigration policy. This means that you are able to bring your culture into Canada and maintain it, celebrate it while still holding on to your Canadian identity.

This seems super positive, but it also comes with its issues: Sometimes in Canada, people can get cloistered into their own cultural groups and not integrate as well. It also means that there's sometimes underlying hostility when people hold on to their cultural values and can't integrate with Canadian cultural values. You usually see this come out during the election season. (The Conservatives without fail will do some whistle blowing, subtlety alluding to racism, or the old way of doing life, but never crossing the line)

More so, often when the "Mosaic concept" is stated, what Canadians really mean is that they want you to bring your delicious culturally diverse food to the communal potluck. Your political leanings, or philosophies on life, should be left at the airport when you arrived.

Beyond the philosophies of integration Canada has a really strong newcomers program. In almost every community that you go into you will be able to find support from Community Services associations, churches, and Government. All are set up to help bring a smoother transition to new Canadians into Canada.

It's also worth noting that Canada has the USA to the South

and West, and a whole lot of ocean surrounding it - so very little of its immigration is "illegal" border dashing. (Not to say that it hasn't happened but that it has made headlines when it did. And it's worth noting that when people did cross on the foot to the Canadian border - not all of it was met with the warm hug of a Canadian mountie holding a Tim Hortons and a double-double coffee to welcome its new people)

USA

The USA's philosophy is often called the "Melting Pot." While they welcome immigrants from all over the world, they also expect newcomers to adapt to the American way of life.

- And although the U.S. has diverse immigrant communities, there's also a strong emphasis on assimilation to the American way.
- More so, there is less of a focused and overall support system for new immigrants.
- And unfortunately due to political influence from the right there has been a narrative against immigrants. And often quite frankly a focus on immigrants who come without proper documentation.This, unfortunately, can make for a more overt hostile environment.
- To be fair, Americans are also along the border with Mexico and other South American countries which makes it more of a target for illegal immigration or foreign workers to cross the border.

The Gist

- Your everyday Canadian and American are pretty open to immigrants. Please don't be utterly scared by my words; however, don't be naive either.
- But generally, the American media can get more riled up about "illegal immigrants" stealing jobs, and the American media definitely plays this concept on repeat during the American elections (which feels like a year long saga each time it happens). Unfortunately, some people can conflate illegal immigrants with *all* immigrants.
- As an immigrant, you will probably have more social system support in Canada, but it's not like a fully fledged system that's going to help you every step of the way.

Questions to ask yourself

1. I hate to say this, but if you are a person of colour, you may experience more prejudice in your immigration journey than your white counterpart (that sentence is the candidate for the most obvious statement ever written). Arguably, you will experience less overt racism in Canada. (But as the partner to a person of colour and a mom to biracial kids, I am amazed at the dumb, unintentional sh*t I have had to witness my more pigmented family endure). So, what is your tolerance for white people's overt racism (America) vs covert, sometimes, dumbass racism (Canada)?
2. Do you come from a more Western background (English

speaking, some sort of tolerance for or familiarity with Protestant Christianity) or not? If the former, the USA and Canada are your oyster, if the latter, Canada is probably a kinder fit.

3. Do you see yourself ever needing the services for newcomers? (Canada) Or are you dead set on white knuckling your way through immigration, or relying on informal community support (friends, churches, etc)? (USA)

4. Which option in this section seems most appealing to you? Why?

15

Johannes' Story

Montreal, Quebec

I stares at my computer screen in disbelief

Demande refusée.

"You have got to be effing kidding me!"

The Government agent's email sits there statically, and definitively: The application for my business grant has been denied.

I am so angry my brain can't even compute the reasoning listed in the email.

I stand up from my desk and I kick a box. It flies into the wall. I am not the type of person who kicks a box. But today I am.

It's bureaucracy. On red tape. On some government box

checker's binary agenda. And my business and life were on the line.

I crumple back into my chair and put my head into my hands. I swear my hairline is receding by the minute. My brain goes back to the international trade event where I met the Canadian contingent: We strike up an easy conversation as I bring up my family's connections in Canada. He perks up, and starts to inquire earnestly about my business and work. He is so keen. Before you know it, there are promises of if moving my technology company to Canada there would be ample government supported grants for research and development. He brags of the talent of the people as well as the deep connections to the States.

It was enough to get me and my family over here. It took so much effort to convince my wife that this would be a once in a lifetime to build something bigger. That the Canadian lifestyle would suit us, and that being in Canada would make expansion to the States a real option for the business.

But being here. That is something different.

The promises of swift moving business deals and support to set up shop have been slower than imagined. Getting to meet the right people to grease the wheels has not been easy. And the government grants that they were bragging about back in the Netherlands? They have been a bureaucratic nightmare. Slowly my capital is being drained and now the entire company is at risk.

I wonder if I have just made the biggest gamble of my life on the wrong horse.

75

16

Entrepreneurship

Entrepreneurs are a special breed of people. Who gives up a 40 hour workweek so that they can work an 80 hour week instead? Entrepreneurs do, that's who. All the hopes of growing something bigger in the long run.

To clarify, I'm not talking about self employment, contract work or side hustles. I am talking about a scalable business where you can step away as the operator and the thing still runs. (Nothing wrong with this, just a bit of clarity for this section)

For these entrepreneurs, it's a bumpy existence: The demanding nature of getting investments, making investors happy, finding good talent, having cash flow, and garnering grants are all in a day's work. Plus the lows are often met with some amazing highs once there is an occasional breakthrough. It is a ride.

And when you add immigration to the mix: This cross cultural adventure is like buckling up for a chaotic rollercoaster with unanticipated detours around every corner.

Canada

- Canada isn't always synonymous with entrepreneurship. But I think it's an unfair image that we have that we are not friendly towards businesses. Canada is like your loyal sidekick who always has your back in the world of entrepreneurship. They believe in giving everyone a chance to shine. Canada's all about supporting small businesses and startups. They offer funding, training, and mentorship to help entrepreneurs get their ideas off the ground. It's like having a buddy who says, "You can do it! Let's make it happen together!"
- Canada does have its fair share of Entrepreneurship. I used to work for a Chamber of Commerce and run Small Business Week and I can tell you that there are some amazing innovative businesses in Canada.
- However, I can also say Canada often faces quite a bit of red tape. It also has taxes at multiple levels of government which can hinder the growth of a small business.
- Canada also has stricter labour laws to protect the worker this sometimes is not looked upon as a friendly business facing situation.
- But, Canada also, has has great governments grants for businesses and innovative research in the tech space as well as other industries
- It's also worth noting that Canada has higher minimum wages than the US of A - which is great for workers, not

so much for the business owners.

USA

- The USA is like the fearless pioneer who's been conquering new frontiers for ages. They're all about big dreams and bold moves. In the US, entrepreneurship is like a celebrated sport. It's a place where you can dream big, take risks, and maybe even become the next big thing. There's a lot of money and opportunity, and it's like saying, "If you can dream it, you can do it!"
- The United States is kind of known for entrepreneurship and huge scale companies and Titans of Industry
- It almost feels as if top Canadian business owners ultimately end up going to the US. I don't think it's a case that Canada is doing such a bad job, I think it's a case that America has a larger market and more opportunities for investment. So the best and the brightest of Canada often end up working in the U.S. market.

The Gist

If you want to be the next Elon Musk, America is the country that you need to be in to make that happen.

If you want to open a smaller boutique IT software technology that's going to get acquired by a larger group - Canada might be the place to incubate that. It's unfortunately a little too specific to the business to know which country would serve you best as a business owner.

Christi's Two Cents

To be brutally honest, I've worked with entrepreneurs to know that those who are super serious about their business will probably do a ton of research to figure out which country and its policies are going to serve the company best. You already know what questions to ask, and have already done the research.

However, I think if you are dreaming of giving up the corporate gig, or the 9 to 5 cycle, eventually, that is. And you are dipping your toe in with an internet, side-hustle business while you work your "regular job"… both countries are pretty equal in setting you up for success. What may be more important is the urban versus rural divide as well as finding communities of *gasp* *real people* who can connect you to the opportunities and networks you need to grow the damn thing. I would research your cities and community, and connect to your local business association for insights.

17

Lienka's Story

New York, New York

I never really thought that I would actually be placed with a family. Much less a family in the States. And moreover, an affluent family in New York City.

Growing up in Klerksdorp, South Africa has a way of keeping your head out of the clouds, and keeping your dreams a bit more realistic. So walking through Uptown New York was never really in the cards.

Everything seemed so much more possible in the land of the brave and free. I loved the children I was placed with, I was taking a class at a college, and everything was going so well. Being an Au Pair meant that I was finally getting to see the world. New York was loud and everyone had their own unique fashion and proudly displayed their opinion for the whole world to hear. I think in some ways I had caught the New York bug of big opinions. I remember clearly the day that all came crashing down.

It was the U.S. elections and Trump looked like he was starting to have a grasp on power. My boss, a classy lady, seemed really unnerved by the whole scenario. She would text and call friends and speak about this was no longer "her America". One day I found her in tears, and asked her what was happening. I was just checking in, the way we would back home, and she was upset about what Trump would mean for the "Pro-choice" movement. She thought it would take women's rights back into the 1950s.

I didn't mean to say that I didn't respect her opinion or that she wasn't entitled to it. All I said was that on the upside there would be more babies who'd get a chance to live.

I can still see her face. The quiet anger rising in her cheeks. Her jaw pulled tight. She didn't speak to me the rest of the day. The next day her husband informed me that they had requested a rematch because they felt that things weren't gelling for them.

I can't help but blush at my naive conservative comment now. Looking back, I just didn't really understand how intense the debate was in the States. And I took Americans at face value when they said that you had the freedom to express your beliefs.

But it turns out there are some topics that only Americans can afford to have opinions over, and if you are not American, you better zip your lip. Although my time in the U.S. was brief, as that was the reality of my situation, I learnt a lot about the power of those who get to have a voice and those whose opinions aren't really allowed to be voiced.

18

Political Climate

Speaking about the political climate of a country is like me asking you to hate me.

So before the hate reviews come in, remember:
1) I am talking about things at high level
2) I am generalising
3) This is going to lack tasty nuance

America: A veritable spicy salsa

The American political climate is very, very spicy. I think things hit a boiling point with Trump as president and it's still very much just boiling at a few degrees below. Here are the things to consider about the US:

The U.S. primarily has a two-party system, with the Democrats and Republicans. These parties can sometimes be at odds, creating a bit of political drama, like a thrilling sports match with both teams playing hard. Except there are no winners and a civil society is the loser.

Spirited Debates: Americans are known for their spirited debates and discussions. Whether it's about healthcare, gun control, or taxes, people in the U.S. are passionate about their beliefs. It's like a high-energy concert with everyone singing their hearts out. (And the pessimist in me believes it's slightly out of tune)

Values: The USA values individual freedoms, a strong economy, and self-reliance. It's like saying, "We're the land of the free, where everyone has the chance to make it big." I once had an economics professor say that Americans prioritise freedom over efficiency. And I was like, "say what?"

He explained that in Canada the ruling to wear seatbelts went pretty quick and was implemented with relatively little fuss. The benefits of wearing seatbelts and saving lives lended it to be an efficient policy that would save lives and lower healthcare costs. So Canadians did it. Versus in America, it was debated and voted over again and again in various communities because of people's desire to self determine what they wanted to do. Freedom of choice is very important in America.

Election campaigns feel like they never end in the US. They have dominated the public arena for a very long time:The fact that the news media refers to it as "an election year" just makes my head hurt. More so, there are so many people jockeying for power, it's difficult to keep your head straight with all the different candidates.

But if I were going to generally paint things: I would say there are two distinct factions in America. First, is the "Liberal Elite" who are spread across the East and Western side of the United States. They also control the media apparently and are thus evil and want to degrade all of American values with botox, spray tan, and sushi.

Then in the centre part of America the "Midwest". (Why it has that name, I don't understand. It geographically doesn't even make sense.) Here the Evangelical political complex has taken a strong foothold. And I believe the people who live here are super nice… as long as you don't disagree with them and you are not the "Liberal Elite".

Canada: Vanilla baby

In comparison, Canada is beautifully… vanilla. Canada's political climate is often seen as polite and moderate. It's like your friendly neighbour who prefers a calm evening at home. Here's why:

- **Multiparty System**: In Canada, they have multiple political parties, but none of them usually lean too far to the extreme. It's like having a conversation over dinner – even if you don't agree on everything, you can still get along. Because truly we are just here to get to the dessert.
- **Steady and Peaceful**: The Canadian political scene is known for its stability. You won't see too many sudden, drastic changes. It's like a gentle stream, flowing steadily. Not to say that it doesn't have its drama, it's just that an

offside comment from the Prime Minister doesn't hold as much sway as throwaway remark from the President

- **Values:** Canada values things like universal healthcare, multiculturalism, and social welfare. They believe in taking care of everyone and embracing diversity. It's like saying, "We're all in this together."(Not to say that don't have more conservative groups that like to rally around issues - with very outsized trucks usually -but it's all a lot more tame)

- **The election cycle is much shorter:** Once the election writs are issued, candidates start campaigning. The election or campaign period must be at least 37 days and no more than 51 days. (Thank you, to the heavenly hosts above.)

Sometimes the Liberals win, sometimes the Conservatives win. Best of all, people end up changing their votes! People aren't hardliners about one party or another. It's isn't a " ride or die" situation for the rest of your life. If one party messes up for too long, Canadians are going to politely kick their butt to the curb.

In the past it used to be that Canada was seen as a fun-loving, friendly, warm, overly hospitable country. For the most part I still believe this to be true - but I would say Covid was one of the first times where I saw more of a right wing, hardliner approach creep in. That is, this mentality that "you are either with us or against us' started to rear its head. And the "us-versus-them dichotomy" generally goes against the very Canadian "Let Live" philosophy.

The Gist

American politics is spicy, and can occupy a lot of air time. Canadian politics is far more tame and rarely gets as much focus. Unless there is a Trudeau in office. Then we get slightly more airtime from the rest of the world.

Questions to ask yourself

1. Do you care about certain political issues deeply? And do you want to affect change in the country to match your views? (Then the U.S. is probably a better fit, but be aware of your audience before you talk too loudly)
2. Would you prefer to just get on with it, and never discuss politics unless completely necessary? (Then Canada is a better fit)
3. Do you care deeply about your choice and your freedoms above all? (Then America is a better fit)
4. Can you tolerate a slower moving bureaucracy and everything having to do in both official languages for legal purposes? (Canada has got you covered)

19

Christi's Story

Langley, British Columbia

I t's January, it's snowing, and my feet have dropped a good six inches through snow into icy water. I am wearing "tekkies" (the South African colloquialism for sneakers), and prickling, freezing water engulfs my shoes and consequently, my feet. And the only thought running through me head is:

"This place is hell… with snow."

We landed in the country about a week ago, during which time we were able to rent an apartment. It was only after the heavy snows melted that we learned we had rented a spot in an industrial area in the middle of a trucking route. On an almost daily basis, a large enough truck would drive right next to the apartment and its vibrations would turn off the TV.

I wish I were kidding.

We bought a second hand car that required the seats to be moved for us all to fit in it. My Dad would use it to get to work, leaving my mother, brother and myself at the apartment. Slightly inconvenient. Slightly stranded. Slightly overcome by cabin fever.

We had heard of Willowbrook mall which was supposedly in walking distance from the apartment. And in our current state of mind, we were willing to do any amount of exploring, even if it meant we walked through a foot of snow (by Canadian standards that is not a lot, by South African standards, that is all the snow that has ever existed in the history of the world).

And now, I was standing in the middle of it, in a snow laden ditch. With the potential of frostbite becoming a lot more real.

How did I end up here?

A funny thing happens when you experience snow in an area you are unfamiliar with… the landscape becomes even more unfamiliar. You become so lost that you have no idea where you are going, where you have come from, and what time it is. It's discombobulating. And you feel like a frightened little child. Too shy to ask for help, because "I am lost because of snow" sounds too ridiculous to utter to a hearty Canadian.

On our way to the mall we got lost. Hours of walking and we had no idea if we were actually any closer to our final destination. So lost that we had to cut through a used car parking lot to try and speed things up. By the time we got to the other side of it, we had run into a hitch:

We didn't anticipate there being a ditch on the other side of the parking lot. It was cold, it was snowing, it was getting darker. We didn't want to backtrack.

And sometimes the only way through it. Is, well, through it. My mother walked over the snow in the ditch, no problem. Then my brother walked over, no trouble. Me, being last and the youngest, it felt like it would be no issue. But the snow had taken as much as it could bear. My foot slipped through the snow and plunged into the ice water. Miles away from that bloody mall. And a world away from the warmth my body knew as normal.

There in the icy ditch, I decided to lose the will to keep going. I uttered to my mom with tears welling in my eyes.

"Ek kan nie verder nie"

I can't go anymore.

To which she responded, in only the way a South African mom can, with a fiery depth of intention that could move mountains.

"Jy klim uit nou!"

You will climb out now.

So I did, we eventually did find the mall. And into a Zellers. (Remember those?) After our traveller's checks were questioned for fraud, they eventually let us buy a few items including socks. Then into the mall's washroom we went.

We placed our fresh new socks into the newly purchased Zeller plastic bags and stuck them back into our wet shoes. My toes were once again dry. Thank God. We walked in that mall with our wet sneakers squeaking against the tile with every step. But, I had never been more grateful.

It would be a while before we could afford new boots. But I had learnt a lesson of deep found respect for the Canadian snow. As well as the starting point for the resilience it takes to thrive in a Great North Winter.

20

Climate

Moving to a new country means that you have to completely rethink your life.

Moving to a country with a completely different climate than the one you grew up with, is just the right amount of change to question your life.

Very dark jokes aside, climate can be a deeply affecting issue as a new immigrant. What seems possible one minute, can feel insurmountable the next once you are in the thick of the long wintery days. I have read dozens of community group posts where new Canadian immigrants beg American Immigrants to enlighten them in living in a warmer area in the States.

Truth be told, you are not really ever going to be prepared for the intense difference in lifestyle that moving to a colder climate entails until you are actually living the experience. But I also want to say that it's not an uncrackable nut. You can adapt, you can figure it out, you can crack this part of the immigration code.

As I am writing these words it's November 14th, in Calgary. My two kids are outside playing with their grandparents in four degrees Celsius. There is no snow, they are bundled, and they are having a blast. If you told me as a child that this would be in my future - I would have also thought that colonising the Moon was on the imminent agenda. That's how far-fetched a lifestyle change would have been for me.

For you, my friend, you may also need to wrap your head about a potentially huge lifestyle change.

Canada: The Cool Maple Leaf

Canada's climate is a bit like enjoying a cool breeze on a sunny day. Here's what you need to know:

- **Diverse, but cool weather**: Canada is massive, and its climate varies from coast to coast. In the western part, near British Columbia, it's more temperate, like a fresh spring morning. But head up north to places like Yukon, and you'll find frigid winters that are colder than the ice in your freezer.
- **Snow, Snow, and More Snow**: Many parts of Canada have pretty long winters, with loads of snow. It's like a never-ending snowball fight! So, if you're into winter

sports like skiing and snowboarding, Canada's got you covered.

- **Four Seasons:** Like changing the channel on your favourite show, Canada offers all four seasons – spring, summer, fall, and winter. You can experience blooming flowers, warm summers, colourful autumn leaves, and magical winter wonderlands. But keep in mind, you will experience winter for up to five months of the year. Which is a freaking long season.

USA: The Land of Variety

The USA's climate is as diverse as its landscapes, like having a weather buffet with something for everyone:

- **Sun and Sand:** If you travel to Florida or California, you'll feel the heat as if you were a reptile curled up on a rock. It feels like summer is here to stay. Ideal for sun worshippers and beach lovers!
- **Tornado Alley**: There is a region in the middle of the nation known as "Tornado Alley." It resembles a natural rollercoaster, complete with tornadoes and stormy weather.
- **Frostbite Time:** There is a lot of snow in the winter in the northern states, such as New York and Michigan. It resembles being inside a perpetually shaky snow globe. Ideal for constructing snowmen!

- **Mild and Moderate**: The climate in the Pacific Northwest, which includes Washington and Oregon, is milder and drier. It's the ideal kind of misty, cozy morning for hot coffee. So much coffee.

The Gist

In Canada, you'll find a lot of cold and snow, especially in the north. Honestly, it's not the faint of heart and you will need to adapt and find ways to survive. I think that the inability to imagine another way of living with the natural elements is sometimes one of the biggest downfalls for new immigrants.

It's also not so bad once you get used to it,

- You have to have a proper winter wardrobe.
- You can do workouts at gyms, community centres and play spaces for kids. Don't let the idea that "my-kids-loved-outdoor-time-in-a-warm-climate-and-that-is-the-only-way can-exist" hold you back. A living arrangement with a basement is huge for that reason
- You have to try to pick up some basic Canadian winter sports. Learning to skate in my twenties and falling on my arse in front of little children was not the most enduring experience, but it did make me feel a little more at home when we did community skate events and I could join in.

That is until February rolls around. Then everyone wants a freaking break from the cold.

However, you can find a little bit of everything in the USA, including sunny beaches, snowy winters, stormy skies, plus everything in between. It resembles a menu with a wide range of weather options.

Keep in mind, there are some very cold places in the USA as well. And you will be paying a premium to live in the warmer climates. Because, well, they are warmer.

If you ever question how prolific the desire for warmth is, my case in point is this cup from Phoenix, Arizona. Starbucks has this series of mugs called the "Been There" series. We pick them up in whatever new city we're travelling in as a memento. "Snowbirds", the term for Canadians wintering in the warm South, is such a part of the culture that it made its way on the mug.

Questions to ask yourself

1. Have you ever lived in a colder climate for an extended period of time? Do you have an idea of what you are getting yourself into?
2. Do you feel it important to get out there in nature and enjoy warmer weather? (Then its team USA for you)
3. Are you comfortable adjusting your lifestyle to fit the colder elements (E.g. In the winter, taking 5 minutes per person to dress warmly to leave the house; scraping down your car every morning for 10 minutes; shovelling the sidewalk; delayering when you get to work; adjusting your skincare routine for winter versus summer months; getting up when it's dark and going home after work and it is dark; learning new winter sports like skating; adjusting your home space with humidifiers, heaters, and lights mimicking the sun). If open to this, Canada is an option.

21

Olena's Story

Halifax, Nova Scotia

"No, I don't think I can do another shift."

I sigh after I put down the phone. A year ago, I would have jumped at the opportunity to do another shift cleaning houses. But now, now, I was just tired of all these "opportunities" that kept coming my way. Or maybe I was just plain tired. I work evening shifts as security guard for the mall, then I study to upgrade my skills in the day, and for a few hours after my learning, I squeeze in some time with my children, and then part time work on the weekend to get some extra money.

When we first came to Canada from the Ukraine, I was overwhelmed by the kindness of people.

Your stove doesn't work? Here is the one from our basement.

Your kids need new clothes, here is a bag of winter items.

Are you looking for work? My aunt could use someone to help organise her house.

It was so incredible to see people rally behind our community after what happened in our country. Plus, I saw that Canadians had done the same for the Syrians as well before us. It was so big hearted of them. I will be forever grateful for that help. I am not sure any other group of people in the world would have been as kind as they have been.

But here's the thing: I feel like I am stuck. The possibility of moving up and beyond this position seems so distant. I can't get a "real" job as I don't have Canadian work experience, and my studies that are meant to switch my career direction to do more professional work haven't moved us forward. It's been over a year now.

Why allow us into the country if we would never be able to join the workforce in a meaningful way? Why keep the fact that we are not Canadian-born as a reason for not getting us a chance to move onto something bigger?

Now my husband and I are stuck doing many odds and ends jobs to move forward. While the city keeps getting more and more expensive. Our rent has gone up $300 in the last year. That is a lot of money to cover each month. And I am just so tired and only have so many hours in the day.

I am grateful to not live in a war zone, it's just I also would like to move out of the small apartment and have a yard for my children to play. Everyday that dream seems more and more far-fetched.

22

Ability to Move Up the Societal Ladder

Here's the hard reality: The one immigration consultants, and even immigrants themselves don't easily admit. Immigration, for whatever reasons you immigrate, takes time. A long time. Not the intensive immigration application period of a couple of years or time it takes to truly acclimatise to the weather. No, looking back, that's the easy part. It's the long integration into the new community, building a network, finding meaningful work, and earning more substantial money. That's the hard part.

It's like having kids. From diapers to the first day of school, that's five to six years. And some of those early years feel longer than others while you are in the thick of it. Yes, in the long run they are all worth it. But when I was in the wild west of newborn wake ups, burps, and blow-out diapers and someone said to me "it's gonna be so much better in six to seven years". It would have taken every fibre of my being to not want

101

to punch them in the throat. Metaphorically speaking, as I am a Canadian now, and doing so would be considered very impolite.

Moving up the ladder, finally feeling like you have arrived, earning a higher income, having some breathing room. These things take time.

Each country has certain attributes, systems and mindsets that can either speed up or slow down that process.

Canada: The Inclusive Ladder

- Canada comes with quite a few social programs baked into its government as well as Community Services. This means that there's quite a bit of support for newcomers from services to tax credits, to general Community Support. This makes the ability for you to move up the societal ladder easier.
- Settlement services help immigrants feel connected and at home by providing cultural orientation, language training, and support with job searches.
- Social assistance programs in Canada have the goal to help people in need, including immigrants. Social welfare and employment insurance (EI) are two programs which offer financial assistance in times of economic hardship or job loss.
- Also, Canada's Universal Healthcare program ensures that no one living there—immigrants included—will be unable to afford necessary medical care.

- One of the hardest things you're probably faced with is getting Canadian work. Which is not to be underestimated. It can be really difficult to do so and frustrating because a good-paying job makes all the difference in the world. And honestly, people would prefer that over to receiving social assistance.

America: The Aspiring Skyscraper

America is literally the land of *The American Dream*. The idea that you can work hard and get ahead is instilled into the narrative fibre of the country. There are so many beautiful "Rags to Riches" stories that it is impossible to make it as if it isn't the land of dreams and possibilities.

The caveat that I would put here is, that if you are a special star you may be able to reach those heights and be an incredible example to other people. But the statistics point to more of the American dream being more like the American Lottery. You can win really big but any economist will tell you it is not a safe bet for your retirement to play the lottery. You will lose, the house will win, but people still pay the lottery. I mean *play* the lottery.

- Community outreach varies by region in the United States. As a way to support immigrants, nonprofit organisations and community centres frequently provide language classes, job training, and activities that foster community.

However, depending on the resources available in the community, these services' scope and availability may vary significantly.

- Specific to the state social assistance programs in the U.S. include the Supplemental Nutrition Assistance Program (SNAP) and Temporary Assistance for Needy Families (TANF). Still, access to healthcare frequently correlates with employment, and the United States lacks a universal healthcare system. Some social assistance programs may limit an immigrant's eligibility depending on their immigration status, among other factors.

The Gist

Even though they may have different desires, immigrants can advance in society in both Canada and the United States. It will just take longer than you thought it would (unless you are very well off, then the experience can be quite different.) Canada's strategy, which emphasises social safety nets, is frequently viewed as more hospitable and inclusive. In contrast, the USA offers a wide range of employment options, a top-notch educational system, and economic prospects, but it also has issues which have to be addressed.

Christi's Two Cents

This is anecdotal, because it's my story, but we came to this country with probably $6,000 in savings and not much else. And over the course of twenty three years we have been able to accumulate multiple degrees, obtain home ownership, as well as savings for my children's future. I'm not sure you could say that for a lot of countries. More than that I've been able to gain wonderful networks of friends and colleagues over the years which is only in a society that is open to newcomers fully integrating into that society that you're able to achieve that.

Questions to ask yourself

It's time to be really honest with yourself and make sure you are putting yourself in the best space for success. Or a life with the rewards and the risks that you are comfortable taking.

1. Again, have you done the research and know for sure if you are in a specialist, high earning field? (Then either USA or Canada)
2. Do you foresee yourself gaining the skills that would increase your ability to earn more? (USA or Canada)
3. Is earning a high end income important to you? (USA)
4. Are you more of a generalist and can work in multiple fields, albeit for a lower income? (Canada)
5. Which option in this section seems most appealing to you? Why?

23

Jessica's Story

Chicago, Illinois

"How far along are you?" The nurse asks without looking up.

"Thirty fo- no, thirty five weeks, today" I answer.

"And was there a bloody show?" she throws the question out there as she continues to type.

"A what?" I ask as calmingly as I can without showing how freaked out I am.

"A bloody show?" She finally glances at me.

"I don't know" I squeak out.

She sighs the sigh of working with an imbecile. And in this

case, that imbecile is me.

When my husband, Jordan, was put on placement in the US, I thought that living here would be a fun little adventure for us. Two to three years of living in a new space. I mean how different could it be, we are Canadian for crying out loud. We had travelled to the States since we were kids, I even used to cross the border to pick cheap textbooks when I was in university. But then we found ourselves pregnant earlier than we planned, and our little adventure was increasing in stakes.

But as I stand in front of this nurse holding my pregnant belly this feels like the opposite of adventure. It feels like terror. None of the baby classes prepared me for those. For how big this all feels and how alone I feel right now. All I want is my mom around to make me feel safe. And to be back home.

"Do you have insurance?" the nurse pipes in and pulls me back to reality.

"Yes"

"What's the policy number?"

What is the policy number? I think to myself. Oh sh*t, *what is* the policy number? I start to rummage through my purse. Where is the card Jordan gave me? I keep combing for it. Did I leave it at home? Damn pregnancy brain. Will this be covered? I start to panic, thinking "is there a possibility that it won't?"

"I do have insurance, I just can't find it right now...?"

Just before she can answer. Jordan calls. I mouth "sorry" to the nurse and pick up.

"The nurse, she wants to know if we have insurance, we have insurance, right?

Jordan says we do, and begins reading out the plan number.

I am admitted, and it turns out the baby is fine, and everything is going to be ok. But I have had my first feeling of what being a non-citizen feels like. And for this Canadian, it was truly, truly scary.

24

Giving Birth

I am your immigration bestie, and I am here to spill the tea on immigration. And you thought that you would not get a section on babies? Haha. Read ahead (especially if you don't have kids yet. Or if you think you may, even in the far, far distant future.) Also, if you are the partner to the person who is thinking of giving birth, read this section as well.

Childbirth in Canada

Canada takes a distinctive approach to childbirth, with a strong emphasis on accessibility and inclusivity. Here are the key points to consider before you think about making mini versions of yourself:

- **Universal Healthcare:** As mentioned before, Canada has a robust universal healthcare system. This means that maternity care, including prenatal check-ups, labour and delivery, and postpartum care, is covered for all residents. It's like having a golden ticket to the chocolate factory – expectant mothers don't need to worry about enormous medical bills (but you still have to worry about gestational diabetes, so chocolates have to be in moderation). This ensures that maternity care is accessible to all, regardless of income or insurance.

- **Midwives and Doulas**: In Canada, midwives and doulas play a vital role in the birthing process. They offer support, guidance, and care during pregnancy, labour, and postpartum. It's like having experienced guides on your journey, providing personalised care and emotional support. In Alberta, where I live, you can choose between a doctor or a midwife for your pregnancy and birthing journey (mind you, doctors and obstetricians will step in if it is deemed medically necessary and if beyond the scope of the midwife. The process is pretty seamless, and ultimately the mother and child's health is the top priority).
- Having a Doula to support you during and after your birth is a cost that you have to cover yourself, unless you have awesome extended private medical insurance through your employers. From what I have heard Doulas are incredible, and especially helpful after birth. Their price range varies from $750 - $1650 in Alberta. But it can also cost a lot more than that in other parts of the country (Bautista).
- In Alberta, Midwives and public nurses will come and visit the baby at your house a few days after the birth. Which, trust me, is the most amazing offer anyone can make you.
- In larger cities, like Calgary, there is also the support of

lactation specialists - which in my case was a medical doctor. I had to go to these visits, but the cost was also covered by the medical system.

- **Home Births and Birthing Centers**: Many Canadian provinces offer options for home births and birthing centres in addition to hospital births. It's like choosing your own adventure in childbirth. The decision is often up to the mother, provided her pregnancy is low-risk. This flexibility allows expectant mothers to have a say in where and how they give birth. And to be fair, most women still choose to have a birth in a hospital. Because, science.
- **Extended Maternity Leave:** I will get into parental leave in its own section, but Canada offers generous maternity and parental leave.
- **Lower maternal mortality**: Canada's maternal mortality rates are relatively low compared to global averages, reflecting the country's commitment to maternal health.

Childbirth in the USA

Childbirth in the USA follows a different path, with a more diverse array of options and considerations. Here's what sets it apart:

- **Health Insurance:** The USA's healthcare system is primarily privatised. As we discussed before, there is no surprise here! Expectant mothers typically need health insurance to cover maternity care. Health insurance often plays a critical role in accessing and affording maternity care, including prenatal check-ups, hospital delivery, and postpartum care.

- **Obstetricians and Hospitals:** Obstetricians (OB-GYNs) play a crucial role in American childbirth. Most expectant mothers choose to give birth in hospitals, where doctors and nurses provide medical care. It's like a well-orchestrated performance with a medical team ensuring the safety and well-being of both mother and baby. Hospitals in the USA offer a range of birthing options, from traditional labour and delivery rooms to birthing suites with more home-like settings.
- **Shorter Maternity Leave:** The USA provides shorter maternity leave compared to Canada. (This sentence may be the understatement of the century) Federal law offers 12 weeks of unpaid leave under the Family and Medical Leave Act (FMLA), and some states offer additional paid leave options. Many working mothers in the USA may face challenges balancing work and motherhood, as they often need to return to work relatively soon after giving birth. If you are planning on a) having children b) work as an employee - this is something you have to deeply consider in making your choices between the two countries.
- **Higher Medical Costs:** Childbirth in the USA can be expensive, especially without insurance. The costs can include prenatal care, labour and delivery, and postpartum check-ups. The medical bills can vary greatly depending on factors like insurance coverage, the location of care, and any complications that may arise during pregnancy or delivery.

But to give you a sense of the numbers in 2023: (Masterson and Rivelli)

	Average cost of childbirth	Average out of pocket cost for those with insurance
Childbirth	$18,865	$2,854
Vaginally delivery	$14,768	$2,655
Cesarean	$26,280	$3,214

The thing that these numbers don't capture is the exception to the rule when it comes to a "normal, easy" birth. (Ha, like that ever existed.) Little babies have different needs, and the cost of a few days stay in the NICU can blow these numbers out of the water.

Maternal Health:

Both countries prioritise maternal health, but they face different challenges and outcomes:

In Canada

- Maternal mortality rates are relatively low in Canada. The country's healthcare system focuses on providing quality care to all residents, which contributes to positive maternal health outcomes. However, there are still disparities in maternal health within the country. Some remote and Indigenous communities face challenges and disparities in access to care and health outcomes. Canada is actively working to address these issues through targeted policies and programs, but still it is an issue.

In the USA

When compared to Canada, the United States has a higher rate of maternal mortality. This is a serious problem that is frequently associated with systemic injustices, disparities in healthcare quality, and access to care. In the United States, there are significant concerns about racial and socioeconomic disparities in maternal health outcomes, and closing these gaps is a top priority. There is ongoing work to improve maternal health, particularly in vulnerable populations.

The Gist

When it comes to giving birth, which is a pretty huge and sometimes traumatic event in life. Canada does a very good job at trying to take the stress out of the situation by covering costs and providing a high level of medical care. If you are going to have a baby in the US, you are going to have to do your research for costs and try to make sure you do it at the most opportune time in your life. And if you know kids, you know they like to do things when it suits you best.

That is a joke. They do the absolute opposite.

Questions to ask yourself

1. How many kids do my partner and I see each other having?
2. Take that amount and multiply it by the average cost of an uninsured birth. In the worst case scenario, can you afford this amount? (If so, the USA or Canada may be a good option. If not, Canada is a better bet)
3. In an ideal world you get to have the birth that you want. What type of birth do you want? Do you want Midwives? Or are you set on Doctors? (Honestly, I think you can plan for either option pretty easily in either country, but midwives have quite a bit of popularity and acceptance in Canada.)
4. Which option in this section seems most appealing to you? Why?

25

Gertrude's Story

Calgary, Alberta

It's three am, and I am holding my first born in my arms. It's summer, so the sun will be up in a few hours.

Sophia is eight months old and going through the dreaded sleep regression. I am up so many times in a night that I have lost count. The crook of my elbow has a rash because her head has been in there more times than it is not, and my skin doesn't have enough time to breathe. So now I have a baby rash.

With aching - and itching - arms, I hold her, and I stand through the window and look toward the mountains. Not that I can see them in the dark.

What will tomorrow look like?

I call my mother back in Germany multiple times a day. She keeps telling me I am doing an amazing job. I don't feel that way. But here I am trying to get by day by day. I wish she was here. My husband says we can hire help, but it's just not the same.

When Felix received the job offer for an executive position in the oil and gas industry, he was absolutely thrilled. We moved into this beautiful house, with all the luxuries that come with a new home in a new city. I found work soon afterwards and we fell in love with our new home.

Then we got pregnant, bought a house in one of the "it" neighbourhoods, had a baby, and now I am here. Wondering what my future looks like.

Back home I would have three years before I could take off and know that I could go back to my job, but here, I will have to make a decision in ten months. I know how quickly that time will pass, and before I know it, the big question will have to be answered.Stay at home mom or career mom?

I know. I am the spoiled girl to even be making this choice. Hate on me if you like. I am fully aware how good I have it. So it makes it impossible to voice how I feel to others, because others are in way more stressful situations and they have to work. But I am here, in the darkness of night, away from my family, wondering who I am? What am going to be? Can I do this rhythm for the next five years? And I feel like I have so little time to make that decision.

26

Parental Leave

Nothing tests you like becoming a parent. It's the most beautiful and most tiring time of your life. Those sweet little bundles are everything, and take everything. And when you are busy with your little ones during those long days and even longer nights, you finally realise that living in a tribe with grandparents, aunties, uncles and old-enough cousins to help is literally the most genius thing ever invented.

As an immigrant you lose your tribe.

I personally felt the weight of this with our first born being born during a Covid lockdown and feeling like we were drowning and overwhelmed during those first few months with minimal contact. I still have pictures of my daughter meeting her cousins for the first time through the glass window. My parents weren't able to travel, but my husband's parents saved our lives with home cooked meals, and doing errands to keep the house running. Even our sweet neighbours brought over soup once a week until we were up on our feet. So even when losing a tribe, I felt the kindness of our community.

But my heart goes out to all immigrants who do this monumental milestone period by themselves. Having family helps so much, having resources can ease the burden, being in an established community eases the process. Yet many immigrants don't have them, and more so, they may be facing an imminent return to work. Thus, the topic of parental leave is very close to my heart, as I want you to really garner a sense of what you are heading into when you do this "parent thing" in a new country.

Parental Leave in Canada

Canada is known for its generous approach to parental leave (well, by North American standards, those Scandy countries and Germany have got it going on!). Canada's policies are more supportive of families and help foster a healthy work-life balance. Here are the key points to consider:

- **Maternity and Parental Leave:** In Canada, there are two main types of leave: maternity leave and parental leave. Maternity leave is typically available to biological mothers and lasts up to 15 weeks. Parental leave can be taken by either parent or shared between them, and it provides up to 40 weeks of leave.
- **Benefits During Leave:** The government of Canada provides Employment Insurance (EI) benefits to eligible parents during their leave. These benefits are designed to

partially replace lost income while parents take time off to care for their newborn or newly adopted child. It's like having some financial cushion to ease the transition into parenthood. But how much money does it actually provide you? (Show ME the MONEY!... Man, that reference is old) Well, the long answer is: It depends. Sigh. I am a broken record.

- The current policy is "The amount you receive depends on your insurable earnings* before taxes in the past 52 weeks or since the start of your last claim, whichever is shorter."

But in an attempt to provide you with some actual numbers to work with, I worked with the median income in Canada in 2021 which is $68,400 after tax ("The Daily — Canadian Income Survey, 2021"). And assuming you live in Alberta, that is approximately $92,800 pre tax. So you used to receive approximately $1325.38 a week in after tax income (Nice!). Now on maternity leave, you will receive $650 a week from the government (the maximum amount). Which is only 49% of your income (not as nice).

Generally though, "the basic rate used to calculate maternity and standard parental benefits is 55% of average insurable weekly earnings, up to a maximum amount. In 2023, the maximum amount is $650 a week. For extended parental benefits, this rate is 33% of average insurable weekly earnings, up to a maximum amount. In 2023, the maximum amount is $390 a week" ("EI maternity and parental benefits: How much you could receive")

Also, I have to mention some generous employers provide additional money to employees on maternity or parental leave. This is called a top-up. (I did not receive either of these because I was working on a contract when I was pregnant. Deep breath, deep sigh.)

- **Flexible Options:** Parents in Canada have flexibility in how they choose to use their leave. They can opt for one parent to take the full 55 weeks, or they can share the leave between them. This flexibility allows families to make choices that best suit their needs. ("EI maternity and parental benefits: How much you could receive")
- **Extended Parental Leave:** In addition to the standard 55 weeks of parental leave, parents in Canada have the option to extend their leave further. This is the 18- months-of-leave with 12-months-of-pay option. Extended parental benefits offer a lower benefit rate, but they allow parents to stretch their leave up to 69 weeks.
- **Job Protection:** Employers in Canada are generally required to provide job protection during parental leave. This means that parents can return to their jobs after their leave with the same or a similar position, ensuring job security.

I have to say this all sounds fine and good on paper, but as someone who has recently gone through becoming a mom, these policies are often "on paper" as what company has to follow. Not so much in spirit. Your treatment as a working mom can really vary depending on company to company.

Anecdotally, I have experienced fifty per cent of my mom friends who get shoved into new positions once they come back to their leave - which derails them from their career prospects. Or I have essentially witnessed the "quiet firing" of my friends from their positions. Which is really disappointing and truly dependent on the company that you're working with. So it's not some Canadian bed of roses.

Parental Leave in the USA

Parental leave in the USA is quite different from Canada, with more variation and less federal support. Here's what sets it apart:

- **Family and Medical Leave Act (FMLA):** The USA has the Family and Medical Leave Act (FMLA), which provides eligible employees with up to 12 weeks of unpaid, job-protected leave. This leave can be used for various family and medical reasons, including the birth or adoption of a child.
- **State-Level Programs:** Some states in the USA have their own paid family leave programs, which provide partial wage replacement during leave. These programs are independent of FMLA and vary from state to state. It's like having different editions of the book depending on where you live.
- **Employer Policies:** Parental leave policies often depend on the employer. Some companies in the USA offer paid parental leave as an employee benefit, which can range from a few weeks to several months.

- **Gaps in Coverage:** Not all workers are eligible for FMLA, and not all states offer paid family leave programs. This leaves gaps in coverage, and many individuals do not have access to job-protected or paid leave.
- **Role of Employers:** Employers play a significant role in shaping parental leave policies in the USA. While some companies offer generous leave options, others may provide minimal support.

The Gist

In summary, Canada provides a more comprehensive and generous approach to parental leave, with longer leave periods, financial support, job protection, and flexibility. The USA's approach to parental leave is more diverse, with variations depending on state programs and employer policies. Access to parental leave in the USA can be influenced by a variety of factors, leading to differences in the experiences of new parents.

Questions to ask yourself

Until you have children, it's very hard to know how you will deal with wanting to put them into daycare versus staying at home with them. But as much as you can, be as honest as you can with the ideal situation.

1. Would you like to take time off with your children during their first year to 18 months? (If so, then Canada is a better option)
2. Can you afford to take the time off with unpaid leave? (US)
3. Can you afford to take time off with EI supported leave? How much do you estimate you could receive from EI ?(Canada)
4. What does the state/province you are thinking of living in offer with regards to tax incentives or credits for childcare?
5. Which option in this section seems most appealing to you? Why?

27

Ling-Ling's Story

Naples, Florida

It's 7:32 on a Monday morning. I stand outside the baby nursery and I am not tearing up, I am not crying. No, I am sobbing. In less than an hour's time I have an all hands on deck meeting at the law firm. But I have just handed over my twelve week old girl to the staff for the first time.

What have I done?

I sit in my car with my hands clenching the steering wheel. 7:37 blinks at me. But I can't leave the parking lot.

Do I run back in there? Pick her up? Do I call work and say I can't come? What should I tell my husband?

We had a plan. A very thought out, thorough, down to the "what colour should be paint the nursery" plan. My entire life I thought that I would have kids and return to work as soon as possible. I have worked so hard to get here. I don't want to give up the law and my career, but I am not sure what to do. As someone who always knows what to do, this feels utterly unnerving. This is a good nursery and for the price tag it should be amazing. But Is this the best place?

Should we have opted for a nanny? Can we still work something out with getting my mom here? But visas from China would still take a long time, and what do we do till then?

7:41

I have stopped crying. I push the ignition button, and start the car's engine. With a numb heart I drive to work. I am going to figure something out. If there is one thing I know I can do, and that is figure out a problem.

28

Childcare for Young Children

Childcare is a crucial aspect of a child's early development, and honestly, for adults to keep working to afford their life.

For immigrants, it becomes a necessary life-line, especially if grandparents and aunties are living on the other side of the world and can't come in to help watch the kids. So the systems in place can significantly impact families, making it doable to have kids and continue working. Or making one of the partners the full-time caregiver.

But how much does it cost? Well unfortunately, that question can only be answered with your unique situation in mind. But we can run through the general options.

Canadian Childcare Options:

Childcare choices in Canada are varied and may differ by province. Kindergarten programs, home-based daycares, and licensed daycare centres are typical options. Because each province is free to create its own childcare system, there will always be variations in terms of availability, quality, and price. As a result, the details may vary from province to province, which makes the decision-making process more difficult.

Childcare is a major financial concern for families in Canada, as parents might typically spend a large percentage of their income on it. Not to add to the horror, but finding a place for a child may occasionally be rather challenging, so many families begin looking as soon as they find out when their child's due date.

The Canadian government, at the federal level, provides families with financial relief through the Canada Child Benefit (CCB). Although not specific to childcare expenses, the CCB offers tax-free monthly payments to families, contributing to overall financial support.

To find out the specific amount you would receive you would have to access the CRA's online calculator. But as a general rule of thumb the higher you earn, the less the benefit is to you on a sliding scale.

Annual Family Income	Approximate Monthly CCB Amount (for 2 children)	Approximate amount
Below $30,000	Maximum Benefit	$1,239.50 per month + provincial government support
$30,000 - $65,000	Gradual Reduction	$1,239.50 per month
$65,000 and above	Reduced Benefit	$900.45 per month (reducing with an increase in income)

Median Monthly Cost of Childcare in Canada in 2021

Province	Full-day child care centres		Family/home child care centres	
	Toddler	Preschool	Toddler	Preschool
Alberta	975 – 1,295	850 – 1,198	790 – 900	715 – 900
British Columbia		870 – 1050		800 – 1,190
Manitoba	451	451	451	451
Newfoundland and Labrador	716	651	716	651
New Brunswick	716	690 – 716	738 – 760	682 – 716
Northwest Territories	910	838	1,042	1,085
Nova Scotia	879	879	814	760
Nunavut	1,215		1,411	
Ontario	868 – 1,710	781 – 1,299	857 – 1,153	738 – 1,194
Prince Edward Island	608	586	608	586
Quebec	181	181	181	181
Saskatchewan	675 – 810	625 – 750	700 – 800	650 – 720
Yukon	850	830	750	700

Note: The figures differ based on the cities in the corresponding provinces and are all estimates of the median costs per child. (Macdonald and Friendly)

United States:

Preschool programs, in-home daycare centres, and childcare centres are just a few of the diverse daycare options available in the US. States can, however, differ greatly in terms of these services' accessibility and standard. A variety of options and standards exist across the nation as a result of the decentralised approach taken by some states, while others have invested in early childhood education programs.

Childcare costs in the United States are known to be among the highest globally. The majority of U.S. states have childcare expenses higher than college tuition! Ouch. The average yearly cost of childcare is $14,760. (Adkuloo)

While, generally, urban areas have higher costs than rural areas. For many American families, childcare expenses can rival mortgage or rent payments, placing a considerable strain on household budgets.

The main way that the federal government helps for childcare is through tax credits. Parents can claim a tax credit for a part of their daycare expenses through the Child and Dependent Care Tax Credit (CDCTC). Furthermore, several states have their own subsidy schemes; however, these programs might vary greatly in terms of availability and generosity.

Here is a high-level, annual average breakdown of the costs per state: (Adkuloo)

CHILDCARE FOR YOUNG CHILDREN

US State (alphabetical order)	Annual childcare cost	Monthly childcare cost
Alabama	$6,001	$500
Alaska	$12,120	$1,010
Arizona	$10,948	$912
Arkansas	$6,890	$574
California	$16,945	$1,412
Colorado	$15,325	$1,277
Connecticut	$15,591	$1,299
Delaware	$11,021	$918
Florida	$9,238	$770
Georgia	$8,520	$710
Hawaii	$13,731	$1,144
Idaho	$7,474	$623
Illinois	$13,802	$1,150
Indiana	$12,612	$1,051
Iowa	$10,379	$865
Kansas	$11,222	$935
Kentucky	$6,411	$534
Louisiana	$7,724	$644
Maine	$9,449	$787
Maryland	$15,335	$1,278
Massachusetts	$20,913	$1,743
Michigan	$10,861	$905
Minnesota	$16,087	$1,341
Mississippi	$5,436	$453
Missouri	$10,041	$837
Montana	$9,518	$793
Nebraska	$12,571	$1,048
Nevada	$11,408	$951
New Hampshire	$12,791	$1,066
New Jersey	$12,988	$1,082
New Mexico	$8,617	$718
New York	$15,394	$1,283
North Carolina	$9,480	$790
North Dakota	$9,091	$758

Ohio	$9,697	$808
Oklahoma	$8,576	$715
Oregon	$13,616	$1,135
Pennsylvania	$11,842	$987
Rhode Island	$13,696	$1,141
South Carolina	$7,007	$584
South Dakota	$6,511	$543
Tennessee	$8,732	$728
Texas	$9,324	$777
Utah	$9,945	$829
Vermont	$12,813	$1,068
Virginia	$14,063	$1,172
Washington	$14,554	$1,213
West Virginia	$8,736	$728
Wisconsin	$12,567	$1,047
Wyoming	$10,647	$887

The Gist

It is undeniable from comparing childcare alternatives in the U.S. and Canada that both countries struggle to offer families access to high-quality, reasonably priced childcare. The strategy used in Canada is more decentralised, with major control over childcare systems held by the provinces. One notable example of an efficient and reasonably priced daycare system is the highly subsidised childcare system in Quebec (Do you sense a theme yet?)

States in the United States differ significantly from one another due to the absence of a unified national childcare policy. While many states—like Minnesota—prioritise early childhood education through focused initiatives, other states find it difficult to offer families reasonably priced options.

The governments of both nations fund early childhood development through tax credits and subsidies, demonstrating their recognition of its significance. However, the effectiveness of these measures varies, and the overall affordability of childcare remains a concern for many families.

In reality, I seriously doubt that most people are going to choose a place to stay based on childcare costs. More so, it's a bit of a moving target if you are pre-kids, with policies shifting with different governance at the helm. For instance, within the two months of me writing this chapter, good friends of ours had their daughter in a daycare which cost them a breathtaking grand a month. But then, a new policy came into effect lowering the cost to $350 a month. Saving them $7800 a year, just like that.

However, after your parental leave ends, you need to have a plan to look after your kiddos. Quite frankly you probably don't have the support that local nationals have with their family or stronger network of friends. So you are gonna have to find a way to make this work.

I want to add that from personal experience, I have seen how having kids has changed me and my mom friends when it comes to priorities - as well as the realities - of having kids.

I have witnessed women who wanted to be full-time stay at home parents end up going back to work; others who worked as the top boss sold their companies and worked part time to be more available for the kids. There is no wrong or right path, nor judgement over any course of action you choose. You do what works for you and your family. I would just advise you that that little squishy human you bring home - they will utterly turn your life upside down. Potentially, derailing a lot of your priorities. Plus alongside having them, you also have done a major life changing move to another country. As Americans say "double whammy".

Questions to ask yourself

1. Have you really run the numbers on what childcare will cost? Did you factor in the cost of a second child alongside the cost of the second also in daycare (or even a third kid - go you!). What is that cost?
2. Before you purchase a house, have you factored in child-care or having a stay at home parent option?]
3. Alongside having kids are two major other life purchases: A larger vehicle and/or a home. Have you factored in childcare costs prior to making these purchases?
4. If you or your partner are planning to stay at home for a period of time? If so, has the idea of part time work been on the table?
5. Which option in this section seems most appealing to you? Why?

Christi's Two Cents

With 20/20 hindsight, I wish I could have started building my part time contract work before I had kids, so that I had established some rhythms and did a lot of base learning before being sleep deprived (Let me tell you, there's nothing more intense than writing with one hand while holding a napping baby with the other, and trying not to breathe wrong so you don't wake them).

With the world of online work, there are so many opportunities to create your own career. And although not all options may be the most lucrative, they can a) provide you the flexibility that a regular job can't and b) allow you to keep your skills and resume up to date for if you choose to re-enter the workforce.

29

Maria's Story:

Minneapolis, Minnesota

"Y ou fell asleep while sitting next to the copier. How should I not be concerned?"

Sheila, our HR manager, has always been very caring. She doesn't just bring donuts on Fridays. She deep fries her own and then brings homemade toppings that she has created and refined over years. There's Shawn from accounting's cinnamon, sugar with a hint of nutmeg. Julie, our receptionist's crushed up oreos and Captain crunch. And for me, maple syrup bacon with some hot pepper flakes. To honour my spicy Venezuelan roots.

She is, as Americans like to say, "extra" and I usually love her for it.

But that way she is looking at me right now, it's a whack load of concern that I'd like to turn down a notch. Less extra, please

136

and thank you.

"Maria, what is happening on the home front?"

"This home or Venezuela?" I think to myself. It's a conversation that I do not want to have. Talking about home is hard enough, and quite frankly I don't think many Americans really get what it's like to have a dictator as a leader, and still have your family stuck back in the country. So for the most part, I skip this part and stick to the pleasantries.

"Maria?"

I snap out of it, "I'm fine, I've just been working a second job to try and save up a little more. Too many shifts and not enough hours. It's fine. I have tonight off and I'll go to bed a bit earlier" I smile in a convincing manner. Or so I think.

Sheila doesn't look like she's buying it for a second.

"Listen, I may not look smart, I might not have the most worldly knowledge, hell, I might not know what you are up against. But I know the difference between a bit tired and so exhausted I might drop down any second. So what is actually happening?"

For a second I feel like Sheila has seen me naked. Emotionally naked, that is. Sheila would never allow nudies in the work-place. The way she is looking at me right now makes me think that she is not going to let this go. For someone who makes her own pastries, she could make a damn good hostage negotiator.

"OK, things with my family back home are not going well, they need more money to make ends meet. I don't want them to feel like a burden. I want to support them. But there is only so much I can earn here, till the next time I am up for a raise. So I am working another full time position at night."

Once I stop talking, I see Sheila's eyes watering. There is genuine concern. She wants to make this better, but she doesn't know how.

"It's ok, Sheila. Being able to work like this and provide for my family. It's a rare opportunity that most people back home can't even have. So it's ok for me for now. I have the hope of something better, a lot don't have that. You don't have to worry."

Sheila stands up. She looks determined. She looks fierce. Now, I'm slightly worried.

"Ok, I'll let you be. But I'm gonna chat with management and see what we can do about that raise situation. Now, you have two options, Maria: have a donut, or lie down on the couch, and take a damn nap."

30

Labour Laws: Work Life Balance

I've rarely meet immigrants who don't have a deep sense of work ethic instilled in them. To them, immigration is the once in a lifetime chance for them to build themselves up in a land of opportunities. It's also a time where a) you might have employers take advantage of you b) have to work multiple jobs to bring in more income to try to move forward.

Here are some insights on what the workplace has in store.

Labour Laws in Canada

Canada has a robust system of labour laws, focusing on protecting workers and ensuring fair working conditions. Here's what you need to know:

- **Labour Standards:** Canadian provinces and territories have their own labour standards legislation, setting rules for minimum wage, working hours, and overtime.

- **Minimum Wage:** Each province or territory in Canada establishes its minimum wage. This can vary significantly from one region to another. As per the Retail Council of Canada the current rates are: ("Resources - Quick Facts - Minimum Wage by Province")

Alberta	$15.00	Effective as of October 1, 2018.
British Columbia	$16.75	Effective as of June 1, 2023.
Manitoba	$15.30	Effective as of October 1, 2023.
New Brunswick	$14.75	Effective as of April 1, 2023.
Newfoundland & Labrador	$15.00	Effective as of October 1, 2023.
Northwest Territories	$16.05	Effective as of September 1, 2023.
Nova Scotia	$15.00	Effective as of October 1, 2023.
Nunavut	$16.00	Effective as of April 1, 2020.
Ontario	$16.55	Effective as of October 1, 2023.
Prince Edward Island	$15.00	Effective as of October 1, 2023. The rate will move to $15.40 on April 1, 2024 and to $16.00 on October 1, 2024.
Quebec	$15.25	On May 1, 2023, Quebec's minimum wage increased to $15.25.
Saskatchewan	$14.00	Effective as of October 1, 2023.
Yukon	$16.77	Effective as of April 1, 2023.

As a side note, minimum wage is not "a living wage". A living wage is defined as "A living wage is the hourly wage a worker needs to earn to cover their basic expenses and participate in their community." (Living Wage Canada) If you are looking to see if an hourly wage can cover your living expenses in Canada. I would recommend running a city comparison on LivingWage.ca

- **Time Off**: In Canada, workers are entitled to various types of time off, including statutory holidays, vacation time, and parental leave. Statutory holidays are where workers get paid time off on days like New Year's Day and Canada Day. Generally, there is about one statutory holiday a month, with some variations between the provinces.
- **Sick Leave:** Many provinces provide a certain number of paid sick days to workers. For example, in Ontario, workers are entitled to three paid sick days per year. While those employed in the federally regulated private sector have up to 10 days of leave per year (Government of Canada). But this varies from province to province, and for those employed in the private sector. Us, regular non-government employed, folks don't get this premium type of treatment.
- **Legal Obligations of Employers:** Employers in Canada have legal obligations to provide safe and healthy working conditions, fair wages, and comply with labour laws.
- **Fun Fact:** In 2022, Canadian employees were working on average 35.7 hours a week.

Labour Laws in the USA

The USA also has labour laws, but they differ in several key ways from Canada:

- **Labour Standards**: Labor laws in the USA are primarily federal, with additional regulations at the state level. This means that federal laws, like the Fair Labor Standards Act

(FLSA), set some basic standards for minimum wage and overtime, but each state can have its own laws as well.

- **Minimum Wage:** The federal minimum wage in the USA (as of 2022) was $7.25 per hour ("Minimum Wage"). However, many states have their own minimum wage laws, which can be higher than the federal rate. It's like having a minimum wage chapter in the book with annotations for each state. And for your curiosity, here are the rates by state.

State	2023 Minimum Hourly Wage
Alabama	$7.25
Alaska	$10.85
Arizona	$13.85
Arkansas	$11.00
California	$15.50 for all employers.
Colorado	$13.65
Connecticut	$15.00
Delaware	$11.75
Florida	$12.00
Georgia	$7.25
Hawaii	$12.00
Idaho	$7.25
Illinois	$13.00
Indiana	$7.25

State	Minimum Wage
Iowa	$7.25
Kansas	$7.25
Kentucky	$7.25
Louisiana	$7.25
Maine	$13.80
Maryland	$13.25 for employers with 15 or more workers; $12.80 for smaller businesses.
Massachusetts	$15.00
Michigan	$10.10
Minnesota	$8.63 for small employers and $10.59 for large employers.*
Mississippi	$7.25
Missouri	$12.00
Montana	$9.95
Nebraska	$10.50
Nevada	$10.25 for employers offering qualifying health benefits; $11.25 for all others.
New Hampshire	$7.25
New Jersey	$14.13 for most employers; $12.93 for seasonal and small employers who have less than six workers.
New Mexico	$12.00
New York	$15.00 for New York City, Long Island and Westchester; $14.20 for the rest of the state.
North Carolina	$7.25
North Dakota	$7.25
Ohio	$10.10
Oklahoma	$7.25
Oregon	$15.45 for employers in the Portland metro; $13.20 for non-urban counties; and $14.20 for all others.
Pennsylvania	$7.25
Rhode Island	$13.00
South Carolina	$7.25
South Dakota	$10.80

Tennessee	$7.25
Texas	$7.25
Utah	$7.25
Vermont	$13.18
Virginia	$12.00
Washington, D.C.	$17.00
Washington	$15.74
West Virginia	$8.75
Wisconsin	$7.25
Wyoming	$7.25

- **Time Off:** In the USA, there is no federal law mandating paid vacation, holiday, or sick leave. Paid leave policies are often determined by employers or state laws. It's like having a choose-your-own-adventure book for time off, with outcomes depending on where you work and live. What fun! 👀

- **Sick Leave**: Paid sick leave in the USA varies significantly. Some states and cities have implemented laws requiring employers to provide paid sick leave to their workers, but it's not uniform across the country.

- **Legal Obligations of Employers:** Employers in the USA must adhere to federal and state labour laws. They are legally obligated to provide safe working conditions and fair wages, but specific requirements can vary depending on where the business operates. It's like having a rulebook for employers, with different editions for each state.

- **Fun Fact Comparison:** Americans aged 25-54 work an

average of 40.2 hours per week, the most of any age group (Mazur).

The Gist

Canada and the USA have different labour laws, minimum wages, paid time off, sick leave policies, and employer legal obligations. Canada's labour laws are generally more uniform across its provinces, featuring higher minimum wages, mandatory leave, and paid sick leave.

In comparison, the legal system in the United States is more complicated, with different state labour laws and less federal control over paid time off and sick leave. Understanding these distinctions is essential as you investigate specific areas to determine the possible nature of your work circumstances. Once again, keep in mind that each employer will present you with an individual scenario. However, labour laws can provide an idea of the absolute minimum expectations. Unfortunately, this is sometimes all that can be expected.

Christi's Two Cents

When we immigrated to Canada, we needed to earn more to build up a nest egg. For a couple of years my parents did their "professional jobs" and then worked at night as janitors to earn extra income. I worked restaurant and retail jobs during high school and university to help fund my education. But with the world of internet expertise, hopefully you can find something that makes you more than minimum wage.

31

Shane's Story

Ottawa, Ontario

I didn't want to live in Canada my whole life. It was just supposed to be an adventure during my early twenties. I was travelling across the world after university. But one day I climbed onto a ski lift and sat down next to the cutest Canadian I had ever met. I even faked a knee injury to get her to help me, and keep talking to me. It worked, and Bonnie and I were married a year later. The world travelling, and my life in Australia had to wait.

Quickly my life fell into a predictable yet happy script. We fell in love, got married, moved to Ottawa, had kids and I worked in government. We were happy and we did trips back to Australia once every few years. Things seemed settled.

Until one night they were not.

Bonnie and I were camping. The first time since I officially retired. When out of nowhere my arm started with pins and needles. I knew something wasn't right. We went to the hospital, where they confirmed it was a stroke. I was airlifted to the main city Hospital, where, thankfully, I had an incredible recovery.

Yet the incident stuck with me. Was I living the life that I had always wanted, or had I just gone with the flow? I kept trying to push away these new deep desires aside: The idea that *maybe* there was more to life than just living in this one spot. Maybe I wanted to return back to my home country in some way? But what about Bonnie? What about the kids and future grandbabies? But the thoughts just kept eating me.

Bonnie was no fool. She could tell something was up. After a couple of months she cracked me like a nut.

Amazingly enough she was onboard! She didn't also want a retirement that was cookie cutter. So we rearranged our portfolio of assets, downsized our Canadian house, while making sure to not jeopardise residency or access to retirement benefits.

I figure we are in the Autumn of our lives and we should enjoy every second we can while we can.

32

Retirement

When you are in the early stages of immigration, retirement is probably the last thing on your mind. Getting a job, a roof over your head, even a bed to sleep in seems way more crucial. And honestly, those are. But it's also a good idea to check in on your retirement goals a good six to twelve months after landing. Revise them, see what you should be aiming for within your current circumstances. Also, it may give you a sense of what you still want to achieve.

Better yet, you have a big picture idea about what you hope the future will look like by not skipping this section. Obviously you are going to have to be open to change because, well, that's life. But if you have a partner, it's super nice to visualise and dream of what you would like the future to look like.

My husband and I regularly talk about what retirement may look like. And I've even opted (as someone who works on their own schedule) to implement a "Retirement Friday" while the kids have half days at school. I use those hours to do what I would like (just like I would when retired.) Bless my husband's heart, he was totally onboard with the idea! Just by talking about it, we started to get excited about what retirement could mean to us. Plus it also brought into clear focus the sacrifices and decisions we were making now to make it happen. (For context, dear reader, I will probably buy second hand cars until cars are no longer a thing, as trade for the joy of work flexibility).

Here is a rundown of some of the retirement financial vehicles you have available to you in each country.

Canada

In Canada, individuals have several retirement investment options, and many of these are similar to those in the USA:

- **Registered Retirement Savings Plan (RRSP)**: RRSPs are a tax-advantaged way for Canadians to save for retirement. Contributions are tax-deductible, and investment income within the plan grows tax-free until withdrawal.
- **Tax-Free Savings Account (TFSA):** Who doesn't love Tax-free? TFSAs allow Canadians to save and invest money tax-free. While TFSAs can be used for various financial goals, they are also a popular choice for retirement savings. There are yearly contribution limits. (This isn't a damn free for all.)
- **Employer-Sponsored Pension Plans:** Many Canadian employers offer pension plans, such as defined contribution (DC) or defined benefit (DB) plans. DB plans are

gold and if you have one, consider yourself a lucky fish. And of course, government employees/ union members often get these plans. These plans go on and on for the duration of your time on this planet. These plans provide a source of retirement income, with contributions from both employees and employers.

- **Non-Registered Accounts:** Individuals can also invest for retirement in non-registered accounts, such as regular savings or investment accounts, but they don't offer the same tax advantages as registered plans.

Canada has a comprehensive social safety net to support retirees, which includes:

- **Canada Pension Plan (CPP):** The CPP is a government-administered pension plan that provides a source of retirement income for eligible Canadians. Contributions are made during a person's working years, and benefits are received in retirement. It's good to know that it's "payable for life and indexed for inflation. While full retirement benefits are payable at age 65, you can opt to collect CPP at age 60 and take a reduced payment. Or you can defer payments until age 70 and receive a larger payment." (Carrick) For context, in 2023, the maximum amount you could receive if you start your pension at age 65 is $1,306.57 per month (Government of Canada).
- **Old Age Security (OAS):** OAS is a government-funded program providing a basic pension to most Canadians aged 65 and older. The amount is based on residency and

the number of years an individual has lived in Canada after turning 18. It is not based on employment years and if you have over a certain amount of income a year, you will have to repay it. If in 2023 you are 65-74 years old and your income is less than $134,626 and the maximum amount of OAS you can receive is $707.68 a month.

- **Guaranteed Income Supplement (GIS)**: GIS is a supplement for low-income seniors who receive OAS and have little to no other income. It ensures a minimum income level for eligible seniors.
- **Provincial Social Assistance Programs**: Each province in Canada has its own social assistance program that provides financial support to low-income seniors who do not have enough income from other sources.

USA

In the USA, there are similar retirement investment options, but the specifics differ:

- **401(k):** The 401(k) is a popular retirement savings vehicle, typically sponsored by employers. (Again, Americans are, like, obsessed with employment). Contributions are tax-deferred, and many employers offer matching contributions, making it a significant source of retirement savings.
- **Individual Retirement Accounts (IRAs):** IRAs come in two primary types: traditional and Roth. Traditional IRAs offer tax-deferred growth, while Roth IRAs provide tax-free withdrawals in retirement.

- **Employer-Sponsored Retirement Plans:** In addition to 401(k) plans, employers may offer other retirement plans like 403(b) plans for non-profit organisations and government employees or SIMPLE and SEP IRAs for small businesses.
- **Social Security:** While not an investment option in the traditional sense, Social Security is a fundamental component of retirement income in the USA. Workers pay into the system during their careers and receive benefits in retirement.

In the USA, the primary government-backed social security program is:

- **Social Security:** Social Security is a federal program that provides retirement, disability, and survivor benefits. Workers and employers contribute to Social Security through payroll taxes. Eligible individuals receive benefits in retirement, which are based on their earnings history. The maximum benefit you can receive depends on the age you retire and your earning. For example, if you retire at full retirement age in 2023, your maximum benefit would be $3,627. However, if you retire at age 62 in 2023, your maximum benefit would be $2,572. If you retire at age 70 in 2023, your maximum benefit would be $4,555 ("KA-01897"). However to get that amount you would have needed to earn the maximum taxable amount, currently $160,200 for 2023, over a 35-year career. (Brandon) That… is a lot of earnings.

- **Supplemental Security Income (SSI)**: SSI is a federal program that provides financial support to low-income individuals who are aged, blind, or disabled. It can be an additional source of income for eligible low-income seniors.

The Gist

Both Canada and the USA offer retirement investment options, social security programs, and old age pensions to support their ageing populations. While the specific programs and regulations differ, the common goal is to provide financial security and stability for retirees. Individuals in both countries have various options to plan for retirement and access government-backed support, which contributes to a diversified approach to retirement planning.

I'm gonna be honest, when I heard the amount of money that you could receive off American Social Service I was like "damn, that's a lot more than I thought it would be!" But then I also thought to check what the average for a retired worker and it is much lower: about $1,840.27 a month (Christian).

The other key thing that you want to remember is that you are going to be paying for your health insurance out of your pocket once you retire (unless you have an amazing retirement package from your former employer. In 2022, the average monthly cost for medical insurance for a retiree was approximately $170.10, and a 2018 study found that 12% of the retiree's total retirement income was spent on covering medical expenses ("How Much Should You Expect To Spend on Medical Expenses in Retirement?")

The other thing I wanted to note is if you are a Canadian retiree you can be a "snowbird" AKA a Canadian who goes to the U.S. for the cold winter months. You are able to do so for up to 182 days of the year. However you cannot live full-time in the U.S. as a Canadian. You'd have to go through immigration to live there full-time. Also, you will have to buy private health insurance to cover you during your time in the US. There is always a catch, isn't there?

Questions to ask yourself

1. At what age do you think you will be immigrating?
2. At what age do you want to retire?
3. How many working years do you want to put in before retiring? If you have a partner, will they be retiring at the same age as you?
4. Are you working at a place that provides defined benefits? Or will you have to be investing your own income to ultimately fund your retirement?_
5. Do you see yourself living in your own home? Downsizing?
6. Do you see yourself living with your family?
7. Do you have funds set aside for assisted living?
8. What type of lifestyle do you want to have when you retire?

9. Are you able to afford additional healthcare premiums and payments on your retirement income?
10. How often do you see yourself travelling back to your country or origin? What are the costs associated with that?
11. Which option in this section seems most appealing to you? Why?

Christi's Two Cents:

This is the part in the book where I would seriously urge you to speak to a financial advisor even if you are not rolling in the dough. Heck, I would do so even if you are. A fee based advisor can be super helpful for seeing if you are on track for the vision of the life you would like to have.

When it comes to choosing between Canada and the USA as the best option to retire, it's going to be closely tied to your earning potential as well as the calculation of age and retirement funding sources. As much as you want to plan for your ideal retirement (a superyacht cascading through the mediterranean sea), also be open to more local yet relaxing scenarios, and plan for those options as well.

33

Mae's Story

Mission, BC

"How *much* more will I have to pay?"

I brace myself for the total. Just how much is this going to suck? The realtor mumbles a few things about it being government's taxes, and that it wasn't something I should take personally. It was just the cost of buying a home in the Lower Mainland.

"So how much *will* it be?" I venture.

"It's a 2% tax, so…"

He quickly types in some numbers

"…another $22,894 and 32 cents"

My stomach sinks.

He continues: "You are lucky though, if you were a non resident buyer it would cost a lot more. Like…"

He types again.

"…$228,942 and 20 cents more"

I guess this is supposed to make me feel grateful. Buying a home is not an option for everyone. But it's just that it feels insane: Immigration costs, moving everything, and now buying a home in an outer city of Vancouver for over a million - just for the pleasure of an over two hour commute to Vancouver.

And then there is my brother. The idea of moving from Hong Kong with all its civil unrest was an idea that he had been toying with. But buying a property out here without permanently living here added another 20 percent to the already hefty price tag.

I guess that's the price of living in a peaceful nation.

34

Housing Costs

This is going to be an intense chapter so screw your heads on and take a deep breath, because sometimes the only way through it, is well, through it.

Canada

In Canada, the cost of houses varies widely depending on the region, with significant differences between urban and rural areas. Some key points to consider include:

- **Regional Variation**: Canada is a vast country, and the cost of housing can differ significantly from one province or city to another. Major cities like Vancouver and Toronto are known for their high housing prices (like scary high… like I would encourage you to move to anywhere else than these cities), while smaller cities and rural areas generally offer more affordable options.
- **Housing Market Cycles:** Canadian housing markets

can experience cycles of boom and bust. Just like any other country. But the last 20 years in Canada has essentially been a crazy boom. The last decade saw Greater Vancouver homes having gone up an average value of 159 per cent in the last decade (McElroy). In comparison the S&P 500 went up 138.8% ("S&P 500 10 Year Return (I:SP50010Y)"). A detached bungalow with no renovations and slightly damp basement outperformed five hundred of America's largest companies.

- Factors like low interest rates, population growth, and foreign investment can drive up prices, making it challenging for some buyers to enter the market.

- **Government Interventions:** To address housing affordability, the Canadian government has introduced measures like the First-Time Home Buyer Incentive and the stress test for mortgage applicants to ensure they can handle higher interest rates.

- **Condominiums**: In urban centres, condos are often a more affordable housing option, appealing to first-time buyers and those looking for low-maintenance living. And quite frankly it is sometimes the only option some people can afford.

Geography plays a significant role in Canadian housing costs. Some geographical considerations include:

- **Urban vs. Rural:** Major urban centres like Toronto and Vancouver tend to have higher housing prices due to demand and limited space for expansion. In contrast, rural areas and smaller towns generally offer more affordable housing options.

- **Provincial Differences:** Each province in Canada has its own housing market dynamics. For instance, provinces like British Columbia and Ontario have experienced substantial price increases in urban areas, while provinces like New Brunswick and Newfoundland and Labrador offer more affordable housing.
- **Climate and Location:** Climate and proximity to natural amenities can also impact housing prices. Like anywhere in the world, properties with scenic views, access to water, or close proximity to outdoor activities can command higher prices. But there is a reason British Columbia is as popular as it is. It's the most temperate of all the provinces.

Canadian Mortgage Rates

Mortgage rates in Canada are influenced by various factors, including:

- **Bank of Canada:** The Bank of Canada sets the overnight lending rate, which has a direct impact on mortgage rates. When the central bank lowers the rate, it tends to lead to lower mortgage rates.
- **Fixed and Variable Rates:** Canadians can choose between fixed-rate and variable-rate mortgages. Fixed rates remain constant for the term of the mortgage, while variable rates are tied to the prime lending rate and can fluctuate.
- **Amortisation Period:** The length of the mortgage term can vary, with typical periods ranging from 15 to 25 years.

(yes, 30 year options, but they are rare). Shorter terms often come with lower interest rates, but higher monthly payments.

- **Market Competition**: Mortgage rates can vary among different lenders. Competition in the mortgage market can lead to more competitive rates, benefiting consumers.
- **Credit scores** play a crucial role in determining mortgage rates in both countries.

Canadian taxes when buying a property

And just when you thought things couldn't get more complicated. There are additional taxes that vary from province to province once you actually buy a property. Your status as a non- Canadian can also play into the amount you pay.

1. British Columbia:

- Property Transfer Tax (PTT): Calculated on the property's fair market value.
- First $200,000: 1%
- From $200,001 to $2,000,000: 2%
- Over $2,000,000: 3%
- Foreign Buyers Tax: Additional 20% on the PTT for non-Canadian citizens (Exclusions from the measure include foreign nationals purchasing their primary residence in Canada, as well as permanent residents, foreign workers, and students. Therefore, the restriction only applies to foreign nationals who wish to buy a residential property—

and not as their primary residence—and do not currently possess a valid work permit or study permit.) ("What Non-resident Buyers or Sellers of Real Estate in BC Needs to Know about Taxes")

2. Alberta:

- No provincial sales tax or specific property purchase tax.

3. Saskatchewan:

- Provincial Sales Tax (PST): Applied on insurance, legal fees, and home inspection services.
- Property taxes are set by municipalities.

4. Manitoba:

- Land Transfer Tax: Applied when transferring property.
- Up to $30,000: 0%
- From $30,001 to $90,000: 0.5%
- From $90,001 to $150,000: 1%
- Over $150,000: 1.5%
- Property taxes are collected by municipalities, including a provincial education tax.

5. Ontario:

- Land Transfer Tax: Applied on the property's value.
- Up to $55,000: 0.5%
- From $55,001 to $250,000: 1%
- From $250,001 to $400,000: 1.5%

- Over $400,000: 2%
- Toronto has additional rates.
- Non-Resident Speculation Tax: Extra 15% for foreign buyers.

6. Quebec:

- Notary Fee: A unique aspect of property transactions.
- Property taxes and school taxes are set by municipalities.

7. New Brunswick:

- Property Transfer Tax: Calculated on the property's assessed value.
- Up to $500,000: 0.5%
- Over $500,000: 1%
- Property taxes are set by municipalities, including a provincial education tax.

8. Nova Scotia:

- Deed Transfer Tax: Applied on the property's value.
- $100 - $150,000: 1.5%
- Over $150,000: 1.5% on the first $150,000 and 1.5% on the balance.
- Property taxes are levied by municipalities, with a provincial deed transfer tax.

9. Prince Edward Island:

- Deed Transfer Tax: Applied on the property's value.

- $1 - $30,000: 1%
- Over $30,000: 2%
- Property taxes contribute to municipal services.

10. Newfoundland and Labrador:

- Deed Transfer Tax: Applied on the property's value.
- Up to $500,000: 0.4%
- Over $500,000: 0.5%
- Property taxes are levied by municipalities, with a provincial portion supporting education and health services.

Property purchase taxes vary by province in Canada. British Columbia and Ontario are noteworthy for their particular land transfer taxes and additional fees for foreign buyers. Meanwhile, Alberta does not have a provincial sales tax, creating a unique buying environment. Understanding these percentages and nuances is critical for anyone thinking about buying property in different provinces.

USA

The United States also has a diverse housing market with varying costs across different regions:

- **Geographical Diversity**: The USA is vast and geographically diverse, leading to a wide range of housing costs. Coastal cities like New York and San Francisco tend to have high housing prices, while more rural areas often offer more affordable housing.

- **Real Estate Market Cycles**: Housing markets in the USA can experience cycles of growth and recession, often influenced by factors like economic conditions, job opportunities, and local demand.
- **Mortgage Interest Rates:** Mortgage interest rates in the USA can vary and impact the overall cost of homeownership. Low-interest rates can make it more affordable to buy a home, while high rates can increase the cost of borrowing.
- **Government Programs**: Various government programs in the USA, such as the Federal Housing Administration (FHA) loans and the Department of Veterans Affairs (VA) loans, aim to make homeownership more accessible for different segments of the population.

Geography in the USA plays a crucial role in housing costs, with notable differences such as:

- **Coastal vs. Inland:** Coastal cities, especially on the East and West Coasts, tend to have higher housing costs due to demand and limited space for new construction. Inland areas and the Midwest often offer more affordable housing.
- **Metropolitan Areas:** Major metropolitan areas like New York City, Los Angeles, and San Francisco have some of the highest housing costs in the country. Smaller cities and rural areas generally offer more affordable options.

- **Climate and Amenities:** Housing costs can be influenced by climate and proximity to amenities. Areas with mild climates, access to beaches, or recreational opportunities may have higher housing prices. Think California, Texas, and Florida. Any place with warmth and sunshine.

Mortgage rates in the USA are influenced by:

- **The Federal Reserve**: Imagine the Federal Reserve as the storyteller setting the stage. They have a tool called the federal funds rate, and when they tweak it, it sends ripples through mortgage rates. If they raise it, mortgage rates might climb; if they lower it, rates could become more affordable.
- **Credit Scores**: Your credit score is the protagonist in your mortgage tale. A sparkling credit score earns you lower rates, like a reward for financial responsibility. But if your credit score isn't perfect, lenders might offer you a mortgage, but with slightly higher rates.
- **Loan Type** : Think of different loans as various story genres. Fixed-rate mortgages are like stable classics, keeping your interest rate constant. Adjustable-rate mortgages are more adventurous, with rates that can change. Pick your mortgage adventure based on your preference for stability or a bit of unpredictability.
- **Down Payment**:Your down payment is the hero's savings in the story. The more you can put down, the less risky you seem to lenders. A bigger down payment might earn you lower rates, like a special power-up for your financial

quest.

- **Economic Trends**: The economic backdrop sets the scene for our mortgage tale. Inflation, unemployment, and global events all influence the plot. If the economic plot twists, the Federal Reserve might adjust rates, impacting the overall vibe of your mortgage story.

American taxes when buying a property

Things get a lot more complicated in America, well, because they have a lot more states to keep things spicy. Always double check the area you are thinking of buying in, but here is a quick summary of some of the state's special taxes. (So special.)

1. California:

- Property Transfer Tax: Varies by county.
- For example, in San Francisco, it's $5.30 per $1,000 of the sales price.

2. New York:

- Transfer Tax: $2 per $500 of consideration for properties under $3 million, $3.25 per $500 for properties over $3 million.
- Mansion Tax: Applied on properties over $1 million, starting at 1% and increasing on a sliding scale.

3. Texas:

- No state-level property transfer tax.

4. Florida:

  - Documentary Stamp Tax: $0.70 per $100 of the purchase price.

5. Illinois:

  - Transfer Tax: Varies by municipality, often split between buyer and seller.
  - State Transfer Tax: $1 per $1,000 of the purchase price.

6. Pennsylvania:

  - Realty Transfer Tax: 1% imposed by the state, with an additional local tax often imposed.

7. Arizona:

  - Transaction Privilege Tax: Applied on the gross proceeds of sales and leases. The rate varies by location.

8. Colorado:

  - Documentary Fee: Typically $0.01 per $100 of consideration.

9. Massachusetts:

  - Deed Excise Tax: $4.56 per $1,000 of consideration.

10. Georgia:

- Transfer Tax: Varies by county, often split between buyer and seller.

11. Ohio:

- Real Property Conveyance Fee: Typically $0.10 per $100 of the purchase price.

12. North Carolina:

- Deed Stamp Tax: $1 per $500 of the purchase price.

13. Michigan:

- State Real Estate Transfer Tax: $3.75 per $500 of the purchase price.

14. Washington:

- Real Estate Excise Tax (REET): Varies by location, ranging from 1.1% to 3%.

15. Virginia:

- Recordation Tax: $0.33 per $100 of consideration.

16. New Jersey:

- Realty Transfer Fee: Varies based on the purchase price,

starting at 1% for properties under $350,000 and increasing on a sliding scale.

17. Maryland:

- Recordation Tax: $5 per $500 of the purchase price, with additional local fees.

18. Wisconsin:

- Transfer Fee: Typically $3 per $1,000 of the purchase price.

19. Missouri:

- Deed Transfer Tax: Varies by county.

20. Tennessee:

- Transfer Tax: $0.37 per $100 of the purchase price.

Property purchase taxes in the United States vary widely. Some states, like Texas, don't have a state-level property transfer tax, while others, such as New York and California, have specific and sometimes complex tax structures. Understanding the tax landscape in the state where you plan to purchase property is crucial for budgeting and financial planning.

The Gist

For many immigrants, the idea of putting a key into a door of a place they call their own - is the ultimate dream of having "made it" in their new home country. And unfortunately where you choose to live can determine whether it remains that - just a dream.

One of the biggest determinations of whether you will be able to afford a home is a combination of your income as well as the location of your home. And if it is important to you, then you should really sit down and look through the numbers again. If this is a goal in life, then it's one that you have to think about strategically.

Ultimately, purchasing a home in Canada or the United States involves a complex interplay of regional housing markets, mortgage rates, and geographical factors. Both countries provide prospective homeowners with a variety of options, each with its own set of challenges and opportunities based on location and economic conditions. Understanding these distinctions is critical for anyone considering buying a home in either country.

Generally though, I think that America offers more opportunity for those who want to own a home just based on home prices being less than its Canadian counterpart. I think that if you have a more modest income and want to own a home in Canada, you should probably do so outside of Vancouver and Toronto. Like *way* outside. Similarly, if you want to live in New York or San Francisco, you are also going to have to fork over the big bucks.

Questions to ask yourself

1. If you had to choose between owning a home or living in an urban hot spot - which would you choose?
2. Is owning a home an important thing for you? (Not what anyone else may say, just you)
3. Would you be willing to look at less "popular" cities as an option to home ownership?
4. Which option in this section seems most appealing to you? Why?

35

Yoruba's Story

Fairfield, California

I t's 103 degrees outside, but I am inside the FoodMaxx, standing by the ice cream section. The coolness of the refrigerated section touches my skin. It is a reprieve from the outdoor oven. It's so hot, I am pretty sure the manager is going to tell me to close the freezer's door.

It's the end of the month. Which means payday. The day I will treat myself to something to celebrate another month in this country. But I am in a weird state of mind which takes away some of the sweetness of this monthly victory. Will it be an "It's It" ice cream bar or a pint Breyers? For ten dollars I can have God's sweetest creation fill my mouth, or for five dollars… something sweet to cool me off?

Three months into living here and in some ways I have started to get familiar with the place. I don't feel lost going to grocery stores, I don't have to use Google maps to get to work, and

I don't keep making conversions from US dollars to Naira. But with familiarity, comes a sense of reality: These constant trades for cheaper brand goods, constantly watching my bank account, and being strategic with gas/petrol fill ups. It seems like this will be my existence. I know that this is the plight of every new immigrant. But I also wonder if staying in this city makes it harder?

My aunty moved twenty years ago, she was the one who was in complete support of my coming here. She said I would enjoy the good weather and having family to rely on. Although it has been good to have someone I know who will look out for me. I wonder if I could ever build the type of life that she has built here for herself? She is by no means a well off lady, but she has been able to secure a small house for herself. She was so positive about the potential of me being in this city that I believed her when she said there would be a future here for me. I can't help but think that maybe there would have been a future for me here ten years ago. But now?

I wonder if I have been priced out already? I don't know if the journey for me here would be as simple as it was for her. I feel bad because she is so happy to have family here and thinks it's permanent - but at night time I search onlinefor similar positions in other states and look up the cost of living. I don't want to pull the rug from under her, or be ungrateful for all she has done to settle me into this town. But I don't want to be stuck in a situation where I can't see myself improving my place in life?

I audibly sigh. I wish I *really* knew what I was getting myself into before I started out here.

The escalating hum from the freezer kicks in and pulls me out of my thoughts. I look around and a staff member is definitely giving me the stink eye for holding the door open for so long. Embarrassed, I reach for the Breyers, put it in my basket and make my way to the checkout.

36

Cost of Living

Moving into a new city is exciting. Around every corner there is something new, and in some ways you get to be a tourist. New and shiny, everywhere.

But with time you will get the hang of it. And with time you will start to get a sense of what the costs of living are as well as your opportunities to earn. As unsexy as it is, researching and truly getting a sense of what your day-to-day costs will be is one of the best returns on investments you can do. Moving to a prohibitively expensive city - when you don't have to - can save you a lot of frustration.

That being said, you are not a tree: You can move if the first place you go to doesn't work out. But I am always surprised by the number of people on forums who are utterly awestruck at the basic cost of living - when the internet exists with exceptional information on these locales. Basing your upcoming move - on trends from five to ten years ago- is a recipe for a painful surprise.

I feel like I wouldn't be doing you justice if I didn't highlight some of the most expensive as well as least expensive locals in both countries. Just because your aunty moved to Vancouver seventeen years ago and wants you to live with her, doesn't mean that it's the best city for you to move to and settle in *now*.

Top 5 Most Expensive Cities in Canada:

1. Vancouver, British Columbia:
Vancouver is a naturally amazing city tucked between the mountains and the ocean. The magnificence of its natural beauty is matched only by its outrageous cost of living. So it's no surprise that Vancouver is always Canada's highest-priced city. The housing market, in particular, is notorious for its astronomical costs. While I was studying there, I relished the understated coolness of the city. But I recognize that I was able to integrate into a community because I was going to university. Which came with its own "built in" network. I could definitely understand how this city without a prepackaged community may be lonely.

Another thing I found very much lacking from the conversation about Vancouver is the cost of housing in the Lower Mainland (also, skyrocketing prices). As well as the naive assumption that one can live in the Lower Mainland and commute to Vancouver on a daily basis. If you do commute, expect a long, long, long ride.

2. Toronto, Ontario:

Toronto, the largest city in Canada, is a buzzing city which reflects the country's status as an economic powerhouse. Professionals flock to Toronto owing to its rich variety of cultures, varied job market, and urban amenities. But there is an expensive price for this. The cost of housing, whether you buy or rent, is a major factor in the high cost of living. Also, expect to spend HOURS on the road if you do any commuting.

3. Victoria, British Columbia:

Victoria, a city on Vancouver Island, is known for its scenic beauty and historical charm. It has a ton of seniors and students too. Thus, it provides an altogether slower pace of life. But this little piece of retirement paradise is not cheap. Because Victoria's real estate market has become so competitive, it can be difficult for locals to find cheap housing. Although living conditions are excellent, there is still a noticeable obstacle in the way of substantial living costs, especially the ones related to housing.

4. Calgary, Alberta:

Calgary, situated in the province of Alberta, is known for its connection to the energy industry. It's also my hometown. So I am pretty damn biassed towards it. While it offers high-paying jobs, the cost of living, especially housing costs, is relatively high. Although not at bat shoot crazy as the aforementioned cities. The city's economic vibrancy and outdoor recreational opportunities contribute to its appeal but also make it one of the more expensive places to live in Canada. Also worth noting that people often complain about the lack of culture in the city, which I call bs on - because there is plenty of it - you just have to be willing to go into the city's core to experience it.

5. Ottawa, Ontario:

As the capital of Canada, Ottawa offers a mix of historical significance and modern amenities. It's also my husband's hometown, and even he would admit that it has a bit of a quieter, sleeper city vibe. But uber cultural. The city boasts a stable job market, largely due to its governmental institutions. However, housing costs, particularly in desirable neighbourhoods, can be steep. While not as expensive as Vancouver or Toronto, Ottawa's cost of living places it among the pricier cities in the country. Again, you are probably going to have to brush up on your French here. But still very navigable even if you don't speak a lick of Francais.

Now,I have given you the shell shocked ticket price, now onto the best bang for your Loonie (that's Canadian for a buck. No, I am not kidding).

Top 5 Least Expensive Cities in Canada:

1. Winnipeg, Manitoba:

Compared to its larger counterparts, Winnipeg, which is wedged away in the middle of the nation, offers a much more affordable lifestyle. For those looking for a balance between affordability and urban amenities, Winnipeg's pretty reasonably priced housing market renders it an appealing choice. The city's pleasant local atmosphere and lively cultural scene boost its appeal. They have the Royal Ballet, after all.

2. Halifax, Nova Scotia:

Halifax, on the East Coast, provides a lower cost of living

along with a charming maritime surroundings. Halifax housing costs are generally more affordable than those in larger cities. The city is a desirable and reasonably priced travel destination because of its rich history, active arts scene, and close proximity to the ocean.

3. Quebec City, Quebec:

Quebec City provides a unique way of life with its European feeling and Canadian charm. Comparing the cost of living, housing included, to major cities in other provinces, it is frequently more affordable. The city is a cheap gem because of its French influence, historical architecture, and cultural events. The downside is that you will have to speak French to fully integrate into this community. Also local government corruption is an issue. But nobody says that aloud. (Hey, it wouldn't be me if I didn't spill the tea.)

4. Edmonton, Alberta:

Edmonton, another city in Alberta, offers a less expensive option than Calgary. Edmonton has generally lower housing costs despite the fact it benefits financially from the energy sector (in reality it's a government city) The city is more appealing to people looking for affordability without sacrificing quality of life because of its dedication to outdoor recreation and green spaces. Plus it has the biggest theatre Fringe Festival in North America, which gives it a ton of bonus points. But, be aware that in Edmonton there is the deep freeze that can settle in, unlike Calgary that has Chinooks (warm winds) in the winter that melt the snow and give you hope to live.

5. Saskatoon, Saskatchewan:

Saskatoon, which lies on the banks of the South Saskatchewan River, provides more affordable housing. When compared to other larger cities, Saskatoon's housing market is relatively less expensive, which draws in residents. The city has appeal because of its welcoming community, riverfront attractions, and cultural events. Also, it can get bloody cold here.

Top 5 Most Expensive Cities in the United States:

1. New York City, New York:

The iconic Big Apple symbolises bustling urban life and cultural richness, but it comes at an exorbitant price. New York City is consistently ranked as one of the most expensive cities in the United States. The city's global economic significance, combined with high housing demand, contributes to sky-high living costs. You can expect to pay a premium for the privilege of calling New York home, whether it's rent, groceries, or a cup of coffee. Honestly though, if I could, I would have loved to live in New York, if even for a couple of months. Because it is awesome. My friend lives as a computer programmer and improv-er and he too has fallen in love with all things New York. Do I hate him for living a life I would dream of…no, why would you even think that?!

2. San Francisco, California:

San Francisco, situated in the heart of Silicon Valley, is synonymous with innovation and breathtaking bay views. However, the success of this tech hub has inflated housing prices, making it one of the most expensive cities in the

United States. The demand for housing in this picturesque city frequently exceeds supply, resulting in astronomical costs for both renters and homebuyers. Fun Fact, I once burnt my feet while walking on the scorching sand of San Fran's beaches. Blisters, people, Blisters! So it's a no for me for that hellishly hot reason alone.

3. Los Angeles, California:

Known for its glitz and glamour, Los Angeles attracts individuals seeking fame, fortune, and the California sun. However, this entertainment hub also comes with a hefty price tag. Housing, transportation, and everyday expenses contribute to the high cost of living. While the city offers a vibrant lifestyle, residents need to navigate the financial challenges that come with it. I would not-so-secretly want to live in LA. For the food alone it's worth it. But alas I will only be making the pilgrimage every few years and live vicariously through watching *Selling Sunset.*

4. Washington, D.C.:

Washington, D.C., as the nation's capital, is a political and cultural centre with a cost of living that reflects its importance. The presence of government institutions and international organisations increases housing demand, which contributes to higher living expenses. While the city has many museums, historical sites, and diverse neighbourhoods, residents must consider the financial implications of living in such a large city.

5. Boston, Massachusetts:

Man, I love Boston. Much more than I ever thought I

would. It is a city that commands a premium in terms of living costs due to its rich history and prestigious universities (Harvard, Baby!) Academic and healthcare institutions in the city contribute to a healthy job market, but they also drive up housing prices. Boston residents frequently face the challenge of balancing a high quality of life with the financial demands of city living.

Top 5 Least Expensive Cities in the United States:

1. El Paso, Texas:

Nestled on the U.S.-Mexico border, El Paso offers a more affordable living experience. The cost of housing, groceries, and other everyday expenses is generally lower compared to larger metropolitan areas. Residents of El Paso enjoy a blend of cultural influences and a more budget-friendly lifestyle.

2. Memphis, Tennessee:

On the banks of the Mississippi River, Memphis provides a more economical living option. The city's rich musical heritage, diverse cuisine, and lower living costs make it an attractive destination. The housing market in Memphis is generally more affordable, contributing to a lower overall cost of living.

3. Wichita, Kansas:

Wichita, located in the heart of the Midwest, offers a more budget-friendly living experience. The city's cost of housing, along with everyday expenses, is generally lower compared to larger urban centres. Wichita's welcoming community and diverse economic opportunities make it an appealing destination for those seeking affordability.

4. Oklahoma City, Oklahoma:

Oklahoma City, known for its friendly atmosphere and western charm, provides a more affordable living alternative. The cost of living, including housing and daily expenses, is generally lower compared to larger cities. Residents enjoy a blend of cultural events, outdoor activities, and a lower financial burden.

5. Indianapolis, Indiana:

Indianapolis, the capital of Indiana, offers a mix of affordability and urban amenities. The cost of living, including housing, is generally more reasonable compared to larger metropolitan areas. The city's sports events, cultural attractions, and lower living costs make it an attractive destination for those seeking a balance between lifestyle and budget.

The Gist

Again, I want to put it out there that it is totally acceptable for you to move to other smaller places instead of the name brand cities. This list is just meant to give you a sampling of ideas if you are completely not sure where to start.

Once more, I want to put it out there, in case there is someone in this world that needs to hear it. You don't have to stay put in the city that you landed in. I personally wish that I had moved from Vancouver to Calgary probably four years earlier, as it was going through quite an economic boom that probably would have propelled my career forward quite a bit.

Cities go through booms as busts, and as a new immigrant with few established roots you have an advantage compared to the citizens of the country: It will not pain you half as much to move again.

Hopefully though, this book can be a starting point to your journey and you can skip the multiple moves.

Questions to ask yourself

1. Are you being influenced to move to a city because lots of other immigrants have told you they moved there? If so,
2. When did they move there?
3. Were they able to buy property at a much lower rate than today's standards?
4. And are living off the dividends of the much inflated prices of home ownership? (Ie. renting a basement suite, second property.)
5. Have you spoken to recent immigrants (of the last 1-2 years) for a feel of what it is like to currently live and find work in these cities? In this case, a more recent immigrant can be way more accurate about what it is like to survive/thrive in that city
6. Which option in this section seems most appealing to you? Why?

37

Yolanda's Story

Brett, my boss, slides the glass door of his office closed. He does not want the rest of the team to hear what he has to say. He sits down at his computer trying to look casual. He starts chatting about the weekend. Then the weather.

This is not going to be good.

It's less than twenty minutes after our team meeting, so I know that's why he called me in. But he has labelled the meeting invitation as a "check in." He asks about what I have planned for the week, but I don't take the bait.

"Brett, are you mad because I said I disagreed with your pitch in the team meeting?"

His mouth moves, but no sound comes out. For a moment, he looks like a slightly surprised fish. Caught off guard with my directness. Being Dutch and living in Canada, this is a more common occurrence than not.

"Well, I don't think it was the best scenario to make that call" he replies.

Ah, there is it. The very Canadian practice of not making waves in a group setting.

"Then when is the best time? I ask blankly.

"Now, during a one-on-one, like this"

I take a breath, hold it for three seconds.

"Ok" I say.

Brett looks confused, but is willing to put this awkwardness behind as quickly as possible. We review the mundane tasks of my week. I slide the glass door closed as I make my way back to my cubicle.

I am five years into living in this country, but just when I think I have a hang of it, I am thrown for a loop when I revert back to some subtly different cultural practices.

I like Canadians, I like their politeness, and their genuine niceness. But sometimes I would just like to say what I was actually thinking - heck what all of us are thinking - instead of having to partake in this delicate dance of making everyone feel like their idea is the best thing I have ever heard. When in reality, it's not. We are not going to do what they suggest, We are not going to give it a second take. But we all have to agree, nod along and quietly dismiss.

But there is something that Canadians don't understand: Being overly polite for politeness sake comes at a cost: It takes unnecessary time, it never lets people learn, because they never fully understand why an idea won't work, and it makes people soft to any sort of opposition. Even good opposition. I understand that you should not deny the value of a person because you disagree with their idea, but I feel trapped and annoyed that I can't just honestly speak my mind if I have a good reason to. Or if I think it would ultimately help the business.

As I turn on my computer at my desk, I reset and repeat to myself:

Yolanda, you live in Canada now. You have to learn to do as the Canadians do. Because if it was so great in the Netherlands, you would be there instead.

38

Culture Clash

I am going to admit 100% honesty here. When we first considered moving to Canada from South Africa, I really thought that we were essentially moving to an alternate version of the USA. I mean, I loved the idea of the States! Disneyland, bagels, American TV. It took me a few years to truly understand the difference between the two countries' cultures. And as best I can, I will highlight the subtle, but oh-so-different nature between these two neighbours.

But to make this judgement calls as useful as possible, I want to add a lens that will give you some nuance:

- Geography matters: what counts as warm friendliness in British Columbia does not look that way in NewFoundland. What is polite in New York is not the same as in Arizona.
- Even within these states or provinces you will see a difference between rural versus urban perspective

- You will also experience a stark difference in the more competitive business world versus non-profit/ social services industry (which I think is true the world over)
- There is also nuanced differences with generational perspectives and outlooks on life
- And then there are individuals who just do their own thing and buck the trend of society. Outliers.

In some ways writing this feels like stating the absolute obvious, but I have thrown so much at you in the last sixteen chapters, maybe this is the reminder that someone needs to hear for the following statements to really land:

Friendliness

- Outgoing Olympics: The U.S. takes the gold in the outgoing Olympics. From high-fives to elaborate small talk, Americans bring the "Howdy, stranger!" spirit to every interaction. To be honest, I got to say I love it. When we travel to the States I have some of the friendliest interactions with strangers, and my kids are treated with so much enthusiasm.
- Outgoing Lite: While Canadians are friendly, they might not do the whole small talk dance as much as their southern neighbours. They're more like, "Hey, about the weather, eh?". It's still friendly, but it's at a level that's more calm.
- Probably one of the biggest examples I can give us. This is when travelling in the states. My husband and I went to a place in Boston where they were serving clam chowder.

This was not a crazy high-end new English establishment. But the server we had was a real raconteur. He would tell incredible stories, engage with us, care about where we were from, and he made a total experience out of the meal. Versus in Canada if we went to some similarly priced place, we probably wouldn't have had that level of service. If we were eating at a higher end place, then I could expect that level of engagement and winning and dining. But Americans generally are really focussed on being customer friendly and going the extra mile.

Politeness

- Canadians are some of the most polite people you will ever meet. I have started to take it for granted, and then when I travel overseas I am very much brought back to reality. They have mastered the art of saying sorry, even if they're not the ones bumping into you. Heck, even I have picked up this habit, and quietly curse myself after being out of earshot. Not. Weird. At. All.
- Americans are polite too, but they aren't gonna apologise for something they haven't done.

Directness

- Americans are known for their direct communication style. If they like your idea, they'll give you a high-five. If not, they might tell you straight up. It's a land of directness, where you always know where you stand. As someone who comes from Dutch background, I have always absolutely enjoyed the straightforward nature ot the Americans

- Canadians try being direct while also being polite. They might say, "I'm not a huge fan of that, sorry," which basically means, "No, thank you."
- Also there is a big sense of saving face on behalf of someone else: Don't be surprised if you walk out of a meeting thinking that one thing happened and then in a follow up email comes along and a whole bunch of different things are stated. Canadians are very polite to your face, but always read the fine print of the business deal because that is where the devil is at.

Rule Abiding

Canadians are for the most part very rule-abiding and proper people, while Americans ask what rules can be bent.

But what does that look like, Christi? Oh, let me tell you. One day, I was taking my toddler to a park in our neighbourhood. The park is also shared by a school, so it gets lots and lots of use.

So we were swinging a swing made just for toddlers. You know, those little bucket ones. Those ones that anyone over the age of three can't physically wedge themselves into. Yes, those ones. When the school's recess bell goes off. No big deal, elementary kids swarm on the playground while I'm swinging my toddler in the *toddler* swing. Did I mention there's only one toddler swing alongside five other regular swings? As we merrily enjoy the aforementioned swing, the lunch monitor comes up to me.

She abruptly announces, "You can't swing here."

Surprised, I ask "Why not?"

"Well, the swings are meant for the school children to enjoy." She states with a straight face while all the five other children's swings are unoccupied and my toddler sits in the *only* toddler swing.

"It's a toddler's swing, older kids can't fit into it" I reply.

"But other kids could lose their turn on the swing" she continues.

I realise that logic does not reside in this conversation.

"Well, if there is a line up for the swings, we will leave" I say smilingly.

"We don't want the big kids to hurt any little kids" she tries.

"I will keep an eye on my daughter and take full responsibility as her parent" I say while my toddler remains tucked in the swing moving through the air.

"The park is only open to the public when it is not school time" she persists.

"Ok, I will make note of the times for next time" I end the conversation. As I know that there is one thing that Canadians can't stand, and that is coming off as rude.

And that's an example of something that you might run into living in Canada, where some people really have a very law-and-rule-abiding personality. But if you question and scratch the logic of it, sometimes you will find there is no good reason that the rule is still there. Like jaywalking, "it's a do not do it" when there is imminent or potential danger. But when it's minus twenty degrees outside and you've checked that no car is coming in either direction, I would go for it. Some Canadians would absolutely not.

I'd like to add that's not all Canadians. I used to work for someone whose parent was a member of parliament. And he would regularly say that his parent espoused the idea that "the rules applied to other people, not them". Charming insight into how lawmakers' brains think. So like in any society, the more power, you have the less of rules apply to you

Verus, on a recent trip to Arizona, we counted on one hand the number of people who wore helmets on their head when cycling. Only after googling did I realise that only those under 18 have to wear a helmet, for everyone else, it was optional. And boy was it ever.

Collective versus Consumer Mindset:

On my last trip to the US, we were travelling with our young children, which meant we travelled with everything and the kitchen sink, plus two car seats.

The airlines are super accommodating on both ends, but only as we were picking up our ample luggage in Arizona, did I think " we could really use a cart (trolley) to gather our many things". But at this airport, you had to pay for the rental of the cart. It was kind of mind boggling to me, as in Canada this is very much just considered a service especially for those who may need it for the additional mobility. This is an example of the consumer versus collective mindset at play.

Later on during the trip when we were going to Target to pick up some essential items. I realised how freaking nice the shopping experience was for not that relatively expensive. You are greeted with carts that have holders for your coffee (each Target store has a Starbucks conveniently located inside). Below is a picture of my daughter completely entranced by the double cup situation.

There are aisles for all your needs: beauty, baby, food, clothing. There is lots of room to move around, and the brands are nice. There is so much more selection of items than there are in Canada.

And again, it's *not that expensive*. I am a skincare girl, and there are products that HealthCanada has deemed not sellable to Canadians in Canada, which are available on the shelves here in America. My daughter is offered stickers by the staff, and she feels great about the experience. Affordable luxury, enjoyable shopping. America, you have it down pat.

I also realise that there is no real Canadian counterpart to this shopping experience. We have cheaper stores and we have WAY more expensive ones. But life's little affordable luxuries are not as much an option in Canada.

But then I would be remiss to not tell you about the time we walked to the local school thinking: There will be a playground for the kids to play!

Yes, there was a playground, but the elementary school was locked up like a prison institution with steel stakes surrounding the perimeter. Why? Because school shootings are so prevalent in the US, that the common public school playground can't exist anymore without barricading the kids in. Which was such a sobering thought and experience.

And no, my toddler didn't get to sit on any swing.

Supersized Experience vs This is Good Enough, eh?

My husband loves sports, while the only sports I grew up with were... theatre sports. The jock and the drama kid ended up together. We are a high school cliche.

But nonetheless, I like to watch sports with him, like an anthropologist going on an expedition. I take copious mental notes of new surroundings, the sights and sounds, the cultural performances and expectations. And I drink wine at any given opportunity.

Within the course of two months we have the opportunity to get very up close and personal seats at a Canadian Ice Hockey game as well as an American NBA game.

And the Canadian game was all fine and good. There was the puck, the players, the ice and few annoyed fans. There was some fun and sweet half time entertainment by little Tim Bit kiddos getting to skate on the ice. A few shirts thrown from the ice, and a few gift cards handed out to the crowds. Normal, simple stuff.

But America was all like, "hold my supersized beer, I'm going to find a gorilla mascot who can jump from a trampoline, do a somersault and then dunk the ball and later on the same gorilla will walk on stilts while surrounded by the most beautiful cheerleaders athletes you will ever set your eyes upon."

True story.

America, I love your sporting extravaganza. Never change.

Conservativeness vs. Liberalness:

I don't love getting political, as I don't want to exclude anyone nor veer too deeply into a polarising topic. That's not the purpose of this book, but here are some short notes outlining the differences:

USA:

The U.S. is like a political tornado, with conservatives and liberals in a constant dance. From red states to blue states, the political spectrum is as diverse as a food festival. It's a land where debates are as common as sitcom reruns. Political debates get so much air time that they have multiple channels dedicated to interpreting different points of view - so that everyone can find their tribe.

Another thing is thatIndividualism is a key ingredient. Whether you're a conservative cowboy or a liberal artist, everyone has their space to shine.

Canada:

Canadians might not have the political thunderstorms of their southern neighbours, but they do have a gentle bit of snow covering the ground. It's a land of political moderation.

Canadians value the collective. It's not just about individual ideals; it's about finding common ground. They're like, "Let's have a group discussion, and then we'll apologise for any disagreements." I kid, only sort of.

Litigation Central vs Nah, We'll Pass, Thanks!

One of the things that will stand out to you as you travel across the states is the sheer number of advertisements there are for lawyers. I don't mean little google ads here and there. No, I mean billboards, buses wrapped with toothy grinning lawyers, tv ads with their own jingles.

It's astounding. Immigration and personal injury claims are left right and centre. It's surprising to me how a country so friendly can have so many lawyers willing to, well "lawyer up". It's a bit of an American conundrum: great community spirit, wonderful customer service and yet, litigation central.

Compared to Canada, where lawyers exist, and are good regular folk who don't often willingly put their faces on moving vehicles.

Cutting Edge Technology vs Let Us Know Once You're Safe

While we were on our last trip in the US, we kept thinking we were spotting google cars taking snapshots of the environment. But we were wrong. There was no driver and panoptic car destroying our last shreds of privacy.

No, these were WAYMO driverless taxis that you could order from your phone and get picked up by.

Our simple Canadian minds were blown.

As that technology had not found it way up in Canada yet. Granted, the added elements of the weather, and getting stuck in a snow bank would cause some more issues versus a drive in a sunny, not a cloud in the sky, gridded American city. But I can't help thinking that the Canadian mindset towards safety first, then innovation second, was also playing a role in this amazingly cool technology not making its way north just yet.

39

Final Questions to Ask Yourself

So my friend, you have come to the end of the book and you are wondering: What is ultimately the right choice for you?

1. Look through the different sections and earmark the ones that stood out to you as most important to you and your situation. Do you see a pattern of the same country coming up as the best option? Which one is it?
2. Now, what are the top three concerns you have about that country?
3. Out of those concerns are ones you have to live with (a law of nature or a law of the land) and which ones can you "crack the code" on (that is, figure out a way to make it work for you and your family.)
4. Now circle back again, which option becomes more clear?

Congratulations! You have found the best option for you. You can now breathe a sigh of relief.

40

Final Thoughts

As someone who can research the heck out of something and then have analysis paralysis, the words of my wise husband are a deep comfort to me: You make the best decision with the information you have and that is that.

By doing this workbook you have probably given the topic more consideration than the majority of immigrants. And now you have a clearly thought out logical option. But have you made the most perfect choice?

No. Because the tough thing about immigration is that you inevitably build up some idealised version of the country in your head. And the reality is always different, more difficult, and more real. There will never be a country that is ideal, because there are no countries that are. Even the Scandinavian ones. I mean they have to construct Ikea furniture like all the time - that can't be fun.

You have done your research now, and you will have to find a way to be ok with the very real and flawed version of the country to which you are moving. Also, as hard as it is to embrace, those first several years of immigration are just going to be plain difficult, no matter where. Unless you have piles of money, which can soften some parts of the landing, but still never takes away the sting of homesickness.

Thank you again for joining me on this journey, it's been a pleasure to share these different perspectives with you, and my hope is that you found it helpful and it gave you some peace of mind. Also I hope that it's not the last I see of you. Feel free to connect with me on Instagram/TikTok at @ChristiinCanada and on Youtube. Or at christiincanada.com

Works Cited

Adkuloo, Neelabja. "How Much Childcare Costs by State in the USA in 2023 | Illumine." *Illumine*, 9 January 2023, https://illumine.app/blog/how-much-childcare-costs-by-state-in-usa/. Accessed 14 November 2023.

"Alberta Child Care Cost Information. Daycare Rates in Alberta." *GoDayCare.com*, http://www.godaycare.com/child-care-cost/alberta. Accessed 13 November 2023.

Bautista, Brielle. "How Much Does A Doula Cost In Alberta? — Doula Brielle." *Doula Brielle*, 10 December 2022, https://www.doulabrielle.ca/blog/cost-of-a-doula-in-alberta. Accessed 2 December 2023.

Brandon, Emily. "How Much You Will Get From Social Security." *U.S. News - Money*, 8 September 2023, https://money.usnews.com/money/retirement/social-security/articles/how-much-you-will-get-from-social-security. Accessed 2 December 2023.

"Canada to stabilize growth and decrease number of new international student permits issued to approximately 360000 for 2024." *Canada.ca*, 22 January 2024, https://www.canada.ca/en/immigration-refugees-citizenship/news/2024/01/canada-to-stabilize-growth-and-decrease-number-of-new-international-student-permits-issued-to-approximately-360000-for-2024.html. Accessed 24 January 2024.

Carrick, Rob. "Canada Pension Plan (CPP) Benefits - Take

Early or Later? Calculator." *The Globe and Mail*, https://www.theglobeandmail.com/investing/personal-finance/tools/cpp-benefits/. Accessed 2 December 2023.

"Child-care costs in B.C. well above national average in 2022." *Business in Vancouver*, 27 July 2023, https://biv.com/article/2023/07/child-care-costs-bc-well-above-national-average-2022. Accessed 13 November 2023.

Christian, Rachel. "What Is The Average Social Security Check?" *Bankrate*, 4 October 2023, https://www.bankrate.com/retirement/average-monthly-social-security-check/. Accessed 2 December 2023.

"COE - Undergraduate Enrollment." *National Center for Education Statistics*, https://nces.ed.gov/programs/coe/indicator/cha/undergrad-enrollment. Accessed 29 November 2023.

Crawley, Mike. "Ontario reaches $10/day child-care deal with federal government: sources." *CBC*, 28 March 2022, https://www.cbc.ca/news/canada/toronto/ontario-10-dollar-child-care-deal-1.6397643. Accessed 13 November 2023.

"The Daily — Canadian Income Survey, 2021." *Statistique Canada*, 2 May 2023, https://www150.statcan.gc.ca/n1/daily-quotidien/230502/dq230502a-eng.htm. Accessed 2 December 2023.

"EI maternity and parental benefits: How much you could receive." *Canada.ca*, 30 December 2022, https://www.canada.ca/en/services/benefits/ei/ei-maternity-parental/benefit-amount.html. Accessed 2 December 2023.

"EI maternity and parental benefits: How much you could receive." *Canada.ca*, 30 December 2022, https://www.canada.ca/en/services/benefits/ei/ei-maternity-parental/benefit-amount.html. Accessed 2 December 2023.

"Facts and stats." *Universities Canada*, https://www.univc

an.ca/universities/facts-and-stats/. Accessed 29 November 2023.

Government of Canada. "Canada Pension Plan - How much could you receive." *Canada.ca*, 20 November 2023, https://www.canada.ca/en/services/benefits/publicpensions/cpp/cpp-benefit/amount.html. Accessed 2 December 2023.

Government of Canada. "10 days of paid sick leave now in force for nearly 1 million federally regulated workers across Canada." *Canada.ca*, 1 December 2022, https://www.canada.ca/en/employment-social-development/news/2022/12/10-days-of-paid-sick-leave-now-in-force-for-nearly-1million-federally-regulated-workers-across-canada.html. Accessed 2 December 2023.

"How Much Should You Expect To Spend on Medical Expenses in Retirement?" *CNBC*, https://www.cnbc.com/select/how-much-expect-to-spend-on-medical-expenses-in-retirement/. Accessed 2 December 2023.

"KA-01897." *SSA FAQs*, 20 April 2023, https://faq.ssa.gov/en-us/Topic/article/KA-01897. Accessed 2 December 2023.

Living Wage Canada. "Living Wage Canada." *Living Wage Canada*, https://www.livingwage.ca/. Accessed 2 December 2023.

Macdonald, David, and Martha Friendly. "Sounding the Alarm COVID-19's impact on Canada's precarious child care sector." Canadian Centre for Policy Alternatives, March 2021, https://policyalternatives.ca/sites/default/files/uploads/publications/National%20Office/2021/03/Sounding%20the%20alarm.pdf. Accessed 13 November 2023.

Masterson, Les, and Elizabeth Rivelli. "How Much Does It Cost To Have A Baby? 2023 Averages." *Forbes*, 1 March 2023, https://www.forbes.com/advisor/health-insurance/average-childbirth-cost/. Accessed 2 December 2023.

Mazur, Caitlin. "What Is The Average Work Hours Per Week In The US? [2023]." *Zippia*, 9 January 2023, https://www.zippia.com/advice/average-work-hours-per-week/. Accessed 2 December 2023.

McElroy, Justin. "One chart shows how unprecedented Vancouver's real estate situation is | Globalnews.ca." *Global News*, 21 February 2016, https://globalnews.ca/news/2531266/one-chart-shows-how-unprecedented-vancouvers-real-estate-situation-is/. Accessed 2 December 2023.

"Minimum Wage." *U.S. Department of Labor*, https://www.dol.gov/general/topic/wages/minimumwage. Accessed 2 December 2023.

Moir, Mackenzie, and The Fraser Institute. "Waiting Your Turn Wait Times for Health Care in Canada, 2022 Report." 2022, https://www.fraserinstitute.org/sites/default/files/waiting-your-turn-2022.pdf. Accessed 29 November 2023.

"Notice – Supplementary Information for the 2024-2026 Immigration Levels Plan." *Notice – Supplementary Information for the 2024-2026 Immigration Levels Plan*, Government of Canada, 1 November 2023, Notice – Supplementary Information for the 2024-2026 Immigration Levels Plan. Accessed 29 November 2023.

"Resources - Quick Facts - Minimum Wage by Province." *Retail Council of Canada*, https://www.retailcouncil.org/resources/quick-facts/minimum-wage-by-province/. Accessed 2 December 2023.

"S&P 500 10 Year Return (I:SP50010Y)." *YCharts*, https://ycharts.com/indicators/sp_500_10_year_return. Accessed 2 December 2023.

"2022 American Community Survey 1-year Estimates Press

Kit." *Census Bureau*, 14 September 2023, https://www.census.gov/newsroom/press-kits/2023/acs-1-year-estimates.html. Accessed 29 November 2023.

"U.S. Population Trends Return to Pre-Pandemic Norms as More States Gain Population." *U.S. Census Bureau*, 19 December 2023, https://www.census.gov/newsroom/press-releases/2023/population-trends-return-to-pre-pandemic-norms.html. Accessed 24 January 2024.

"What Non-resident Buyers or Sellers of Real Estate in BC Needs to Know about Taxes." *Taylor Janis Workplace Law*, 18 April 2023, https://www.tjworkplacelaw.com/blog/bc/what-non-resident-buyers-or-sellers-of-real-estate-in-bc-needs-to-know-about-taxes/. Accessed 19 November 2023.